Homeschooling
in America and in Europe

Edited by John Warwick Montgomery

Pädagogik in Europa in Geschichte und Zukunft / Pedagogy in Europe: The Past and The Future

Volume 6

Homeschooling
in America and in Europe:

A Litmus Test of Democracy

Papers presented by John Warwick Montgomery, Thomas
Schirrmacher and Michael P. Donnelly at the XXV World Congress
of Philosophy of Law and Social Philosophy 15–20 August, 2011, at
Goethe University, Frankfurt am Main, Germany

Edited by John Warwick Montgomery

Foreword by Michael P. Farris

Preface by the Hon. Dallas Miller

WIPF & STOCK · Eugene, Oregon

Verlag für Kultur und Wissenschaft
Culture and Science Publ.
Dr. Thomas Schirrmacher
Bonn 2012

HOMESCHOOLING IN AMERICAN AND IN EUROPE
A Litmus Test of Democracy

This edition published by Wipf and Stock Publishers in cooperation with Verlag für Kultur und Wissenschaft.

Wipf & Stock
An imprint of Wipf and Stock Publishers
199 W. 8th Avenue, Suite 3
Eugene OR, 97401
www.wipfandstock.com

ISBN 13: 978-1-49826-954-4

Manufactured in the U.S.A.

Table of Contents

Foreword

The modern human rights movement arose from the ashes of World War II with a hope that governments would be precluded from ever again denying those rights that are essential to human dignity. It is instructive to look at the scope of these declarations of rights and ask: Why were the proclamations of rights so very broad? The answer should be obvious.

Broad declarations were a necessary and proportional response to the cruel and massive invasion of human dignity that the world just witnessed. A series of human rights instruments in this era affirmed the fundamental nature of the right of parents to choose their children's education.

In the Universal Declaration of Human Rights (1948), the unanimous General Assembly proclaimed: "Parents have a prior right to choose the kind of education that shall be given to their children." There can be no doubt of the meaning of this statement. Parental choice in education must be first in time and first in importance—the State cannot usurp this right without committing a human rights violation.

Just twelve years later, Article 5(b) of the Convention against Discrimination in Education reinforced the necessity of parental choice in education.

> It is essential to respect the liberty of parents and, where applicable, of legal guardians, firstly to choose for their children institutions other than those maintained by the public authorities but conforming to such minimum educational standards as may be laid down or approved by the competent authorities and, secondly, to ensure in a manner consistent with the procedures followed in the State for the application of its legislation. . . .

Yes, governments may require minimal educational standards to ensure that students learn—but states cannot ban private institutions entirely. If the reasonable standards of literacy are met—the State must permit alternative educational systems.

Both of the twin covenants of 1966 contain unmistakable declarations of parental choice in education as a fundamental human right.

Art. 18(3) of the International Covenant on Economic, Social and Cultural Rights contains a nearly verbatim quotation of the just-quoted provision from the Covenant against Discrimination. Parental choice in academic education was specifically affirmed in the world's most basic binding treaty in the economic, social, and cultural sphere. And the ICCPR reinforced the protected nature of the parental role as in moral and religious education in Article 18(4).

And in Europe, Article 2 of the European Convention on Human Rights says plainly:

> In the exercise of any functions which it assumes in relation to education and to teaching, the State shall respect the right of parents to ensure such education and teaching in conformity with their own religions and philosophical convictions.

In light of these repeated declarations of the fundamental human right to choose parentally-directed education, why have Germany, Sweden and a few other nations chosen to pursue draconian policies against families who believe that homeschooling is best for their children? If these governments—like so many American states—erected reasonable policies to ensure that students receive a proper scope and sequence of courses and are periodically evaluated to insure progress, no human rights questions would arise.

In these nations homeschooling is repressed not over concern for the progress of individual children but rather because of the State's view that it, instead of parents, is responsible for the transmission of "democratic values".

Fear of "parallel societies" is what drives the ban on homeschooling. Let's see this for what it really is. It is fear of pluralism. We cannot tolerate elements within our society that differ too much from the norm. Isn't that the very fear that led to massive assault on human rights in the first half of the 20th Century?

Although not everyone may perceive the threat, everyone who believes in protecting human rights should be alarmed. If a few families—who are otherwise willing to demonstrate the academic adequacy of their children's home education—are not tolerated because of this fear of pluralism—who then is truly safe?

Michael P. Farris, J.D., LL.M.
Chancellor, Patrick Henry College
Virginia, U.S.A.

Preface

Those who care for the natural family, parental rights, and the right to homeschool can find principles in international conventions and declarations that support their view. The following excerpts from various international instruments are noteworthy:

1. International Covenant on Civil and Political Rights, Article 23 (1): The family is the natural and fundamental group unit of society and is entitled to protection by society and the State.
2. American Convention on Human Rights, Article 17(1): The family is the natural and fundamental group unit of society and is entitled to protection by society and the State.
3. European Convention of Human Rights, Article 8(1): Everyone has the right to respect for his private and family life, his home, and his correspondence
4. Universal Declaration of Human Rights, Article 25 (3): Parents shall have a prior right to choose the kind of education that shall be given to their children.
5. Declaration on Religious Discrimination, Article 5(1): The parents or, as the case may be, the legal guardian of the child have the right to organize the life within the family in accordance with their religion or belief and bearing in mind the moral education in which they believe the child should be brought up; and Article 5(2) Every child shall enjoy the right to have access to education in the matter of religion or belief in accordance with the wishes of his parents or, as the case may be, legal guardian and shall not be compelled to receive teaching in religion or belief against the wishes of his parents or legal guardians, the best interests of the child being the guiding principle.

The Canadian legal scene illustrates, however, that these internationally guaranteed protections can be and are being disregarded. Here are three cases illustrating how the State can override parental interests, and thus the best interests of the child, in the matter of homeschooling. These cases illustrate how the autonomous-child-rights philosophy works in opposition to the positive statements about the importance of parents and the family in international law. These cases and philosophy can negatively impact the family and define religion as being in opposition to the State and its goals, while ignoring the right of private property.

Case Number 1: Newfoundland

C.R.B. & S.G.B. v. Director of Child Welfare (NFLD) (1995) 428 A.P.R. 1.
This case involved a family in the province of Newfoundland, who have
three children, two of whom were of compulsory school age. As adherents
of the Seventh Day Adventist Church, this family opted to educate their
children at home, in large part to make sure their children received a faith-
based education. The parents had approached two school boards to have
their homeschooling program certified, but the boards denied their request
without reasons. The parents were then charged with truancy and ordered
to send their children to their local government school. Upon their refusal
to send their children to school, the government obtained an ex parte order,
which empowered a social worker to come onto their property and
apprehend all three children and remove them from their parent's care and
place them in government foster care. The court at the first instance (while
the family had no legal representation) ordered that the children be placed
in foster care for four reasons:

1. The family was deemed by the judge to not be providing a form of
   education "approved for children in the province of Newfoundland."
2. The parents had failed to provide immunization shots to their children
   and had kept their children on a strict vegetarian diet. The children by
   all accounts were healthy, but the court felt it was "fundamentally
   important that the children be immunized . . . one of the most important
   areas of concern for those in the public health field."
3. The father's strict adherence to the Bible put the children at risk of
   abuse.
4. The parents sought to pass on their beliefs to their children with a
   dangerous religious zealotry and fervor.

Without the benefit of legal counsel at the first trial and faced with their
children being removed by court order, the family then contacted Home
School Legal Defence Association of Canada and immediate steps were
taken to launch an appeal. The appeal court did not have the same
presumption in favour of State action and autonomous rights for children.
On the four grounds that the trial judge used to remove the children from
the parents care, the appeal court decided as follows:

1. Education of the Children

The appeal court found no evidence that the children's religious education had impacted negatively upon them, nor had the State established that the family's educational program was inadequate. The court found that in light of the fact that there was no evidence on this issue, the onus on the director of child welfare, which was a substantial one, had not been met.

2. Health and medical considerations

Again, the State had not established any evidence that the refusal of the parents to immunize their children constituted any harm. The parents had declared that their children were rarely, if ever, ill, which prompted the appeal court to comment that "this might lead one to the conclusion that the family's dietary regime is in fact healthier than the standard North American diet."

3. Possibility of physical and mental abuse

The appeal court commented that Canadian law recognized corporal punishment as a parental choice where appropriate and that there was no evidentiary basis that the children were either physically or mentally abused.

4. Religious zealotry and fervor

The parents' rather strong apocalyptic beliefs did not fall outside of the purview of constitutional protection for freedom of conscience and religion. Once again, in view of the lack of evidence, the appeal court was prepared to exercise its presumption in favour of the parents and not in favour of the State.

By exercising that presumption, the judge ruled in favour of the family on all four points and ordered the children be returned to the parents' care immediately.

Case Number 2: Nova Scotia

Family and Children's Services of Cumberland County (Nova Scotia) v. G.C. & C.C. (1998) 519 A.P.R. 324. The provincial family and children's service department, through one of its social workers, attempted to gain entry and access to a private residence of the family and demanded an opportunity to interrogate their seven children because of "concerns" with respect to the welfare of the children. The parents politely but firmly rebuffed the attempts by the State to intrude upon the home and interrogate the children. The parents did offer evidence that answered the social worker's concerns, but did not accede to further intrusion in their home. Nevertheless, the State proceeded to ask the family court for an order to gain access and entry to the home and interview the children. The principle concerns of the social worker included the fact that the children were being homeschooled out of religious motivation, corporal discipline was used by the parents, and that the care, upbringing, and neglect of the seven children was a concern because two of the children had problems with bed-wetting. The concern was also expressed about a delay in obtaining medical treatment for the children. This concern was expressed to the court notwithstanding the fact that the family had submitted a doctor's report verifying that all seven children were in fine health.

In this case, the court heard both sides and found that the parents were "different than many parents" because "they have elected to provide formal education themselves for the children: rather than send them to government schools," but this difference did not warrant State intrusion upon their home, nor interruption of their family life and interrogation of their children. Indeed, in dismissing the State's application, the court quoted from the Supreme Court of Canada which encapsulates much of the Western traditional legal view of the family:

> . . . our society is far from having repudiated the privileged role parents exercise in the up bringing of their children. This role translates into a protected sphere of parental-decision making which is coated in the presumption that parents should make important decisions affecting their children, both because parents are more likely to appreciate the best interests of their children and because the state is ill-equipped to make such decisions itself. Moreover, individuals have a deep, personal interest as parents in fostering the growth of their children." (*B.(R) v. Children's Aid Society of Metropolitan Toronto* (1995) 9 R.F.L. (4th) 157 at 207)

Case Number 3: Ontario

In Children's Aid Society for Huron County v. R.B. & J. B (Unreported decision of Ontario Provincial Court Family Division—Madam Justice E. Schnall, October 12, 1999) the Ontario Children's Aid Society received an anonymous letter clearly showing a bias against the family's choice to homeschool their children and subsequently commenced an extensive investigation against the family, who had 11 children at the time. The mother was expecting her twelfth child in August 1999.

When a social worker visited the family, the father consented to her viewing the home to satisfy her that there were no reasons for concern. The social worker insisted that she had the right to interview the children and interrogate them about a complaint based on hearsay and not independently verified. When the family insisted on their privacy and refused to cooperate, the reaction of the Children's Aid Society was to bring an immediate court application for an order asking for the following:

1) That the parents cooperate with the Children's Aid Society;
2) That the Society have independent and private access to the children;
3) That the parents allow the health unit and building inspector into their home;
4) That the parents provide consents as requested by the Society.

To follow their religious beliefs and to protect their children, this family refused to have the children subjected to an interrogation process by the Children's Aid Society workers. Despite receiving substantial reference material on behalf of the family, medical information, and positive character references, the Children's Aid Society continued to press the issue.

The court ruled that because the family "appear to follow a path in life that would be seen by many to be different from the so-called norm, and in that path in their life they resist intrusion by the Children's Aid Society . . . the Court cannot draw a negative inference merely from the stance that they have taken." The Court ruled that it could not draw an adverse inference when parents insist on exercising their constitutional rights and resist State intrusion which is not grounded on anything more than unsubstantiated hearsay. It is significant that the original investigation included a thorough interview by the social worker of the father resulting in an expression of concern that the church the family attended was "evangelical."

The philosophy that "the State knows what is best for children" permeates the investigations of social workers—the cases outlined above being only representative samples. This philosophy is not unique to the Canadian context but is also reflected in the judgments of the treaty monitoring committee established under the United Nations Convention on the Rights of the Child. Each participating nation is affected by this philosophy that works against parents, the family, and ultimately the right to homeschool.

It should thus be evident how timely the present book is for the international advancement of the right of parents to homeschool their children. In the first chapter, Mike Donnelly, an attorney with Home School Legal Defense Association, does a superb job of summarizing the decades-long battle for parental rights in the context of the United States. While currently the U.S. is among the freest nations in the world in which to homeschool, American homeschooling parents did face obstacles when the modern homeschool movement began. These obstacles were eventually overcome with strong and focused advocacy. This advocacy that has created a homeschool friendly nation in the United States was multifaceted: in the courts, in the legislatures and in the area of research and social science—and, most importantly, in the results and product of home education in the children themselves. Donnelly has successfully summarized what transpired in America to ensure that parents have the right to homeschool and that children are not merely creatures of the State.

Educational freedom for parents does not operate in every democratic country. Parents in Germany suffer from an almost totalitarian approach to compulsory school attendance. Thomas Schirrmacher, a leading German theologian and religious freedom advocate, chronicles the struggles of several families in Germany to homeschool their children. This is virtually impossible owing to a long history of compulsory education going back to the 18th century and the tightening of that law by the National Socialists in 1938. The crime created by the Nazis prior to World War II has not been lessened even today. While the struggle of German parents to homeschool seems insurmountable, they have much to learn from American advocates in this area. Dr. Schirrmacher illustrates the benefits of homeschooling as found by German researchers, and this will be most useful for advocates to take to the courts and legislatures. True pluralism and democracy will allow for freedom for parents to homeschool in Germany. This is the bright beam of hope portrayed by Dr. Schirrmacher in an otherwise bleak description of the struggle to homeschool in Germany.

The jurisprudential basis for the right to homeschool in the context of the European Court of Human Rights is profiled in the final chapter. Dr. John Warwick Montgomery is a human rights scholar and advocate in France and the United Kingdom who works with the European Convention on Human Rights in laying the groundwork for successful homeschooling litigation in the European context. This is so very important because the ECHR is the vanguard of international human rights protections. As well, Montgomery shows where some early attempts to use the European Convention to advance homeschooling were doomed to fail and what can be done to more appropriately advocate in this area. True educational pluralism is what nations in Europe must maintain and thereby allow parents the freedom to homeschool. This chapter is valuable for advocates who will undoubtedly take cases through the national courts in European nations and eventually to the ECHR.

Freedom is never established and maintained without strong advocacy. Decision makers and courts at all levels depend on good advocacy. Strong advocacy requires solid academic resources. This book, to my knowledge is one of the first legal and academic works in the area of the international human right to homeschool and it is a rich resource. It assists the advocate and education official in the international context to see that homeschooling of children by their parents is a human right that should be honoured and respected. As national courts look increasingly to resources outside of their domestic context, this work will also be of assistance to advocates of homeschooling in various countries around the world that do not yet have true homeschool freedom. The editor of this volume is to be commended for bringing this work into the legal academic world.

The Honourable Dallas K. Miller
Court of Queen's Bench of Alberta
Lethbridge, Alberta, Canada

Creature of the State?

Homeschooling, the Law, Human Rights, and Parental Autonomy

by Michael P. Donnelly

Introduction

This paper examines the relationship and appropriate demarcation between parental and State authority within the context of modern homeschooling and its 40-year history in the United States. In evaluating these relationships, we review current and historical paradigms and philosophies in North America and Europe regarding the role of the State in education, particularly homeschooling. We will look at how these paradigms have created regulatory frameworks today and the impact that these paradigms have had on the role of the State in education. We will also evaluate these paradigms from the perspective of modern human rights norms articulated in post-1945 human rights conventions. From this, we will conclude that not only is homeschooling a vibrant and effective, albeit controversial, method of education, but also that it demands acceptance under those norms.

We look to the U.S. primarily because homeschooling is an increasingly popular educational alternative with an estimated two million homeschooled children comprising between 3 and 4 percent of the school-age population.[1] Frequent legislative and court controversies over homeschooling reflect the friction that has accompanied the growth of the homeschooling movement. Initially, between 1929 and 1980, controversies were few, with only half a dozen court cases arising over the issue of parents teaching their children at home and not sending them to a state-approved school. However, as the movement grew, court and legislative conflicts occurred annually in every state and became increasingly frequent. These controversies expose the underlying conflict between

---

[1]   Brian D. Ray, *2.04 Million Homeschool Students in the United States in 2010* (Salem, OR: National Home Education Research Institute, 2011), http://www.nheri.org/HomeschoolPopulationReport2010.pdf (accessed May 17, 2011).

competing views on the relationship between families and the State in the area of education.

In evaluating the continuum of possible relationships between State and parents, there are two poles—one where the State has absolute authority to prohibit or prescribe education for children, the other where the State defers almost exclusively to parental authority. The former scheme has been true at certain times in certain societies in history. However, the latter scheme has been the more traditional norm in world history as parents have been traditionally viewed by society as the natural guardians and educators of their children. The tension between the State and parents regarding the education of children can be seen from ancient times. For example, in Sparta, boys were taken from their parents at around age seven and handed over to "schools" to be turned into soldiers to defend the State from its enemies. In ancient Greece, Plato, Socrates, and Aristotle all viewed education as a critical component of perfecting the ideal political entity.[2] However, with the rise of the modern nation-state and the increasing importance of education in our technology-driven world, issues over the demarcation of authority between parents and the State have become increasingly complex with tension between the State and parents running high at times.

These issues come sharply into focus in the homeschool setting. Parental influence is at its height when homeschooling. In a homeschool setting parents direct most, if not all, educational activities. They also establish the pedagogical, philosophical, religious, and overall educational framework in which children learn. Even where the State mandates curriculum and assessment mechanisms, the parents are supreme in influencing their child's worldview comprised of beliefs, values, politics, morality, religion, and more. In the homeschool setting, the State's influence in these areas is severely limited; to those who believe that it is the proper role of the State to "socialize" (read: influence the development of a child's worldview), this is cited as a cause for great concern.

One's beliefs about the State's role in education are influenced by one's views regarding the primary role of the State in society overall. Strong proponents of the State influencing and shaping society have no choice but to argue, as will be shown herein, that the State must take a leading role in educating children. After all, children *are* the future of the society and of the State. Indeed, if the State *is responsible* for education or has a significant interest therein, then it *must* have broad authority by which to

---

[2]   Nathan Tarcov, *Locke's Education for Liberty* (Chicago: University of Chicago Press, 1984), 2.

prescribe the method, mechanism, and acceptable outcomes of education; it must also be able to review and enforce these desired outcomes. If parents, on the other hand, are responsible, then it is the State's duty to defer to parents absent a compelling reason to interfere.[3]

Much of the controversy over parental autonomy in education, and particularly reflected in homeschooling, is about where, how, and, in some cases, *if* these boundaries between State and parents should be drawn. Some argue that the State has no role in education, or, if any, a minimal one. They often recognize that the State may establish a public education system if it so desires and may, because it has the power to do so, even confiscate money through taxation to pay for it. But, they say, the State may *not* require a child to be subjected to the public education system contrary to a parent's convictions. This is the current law in America pursuant to United States Supreme Court jurisprudence. On the other hand, others argue that every child has a right to education and must receive a State-approved and State-funded educational experience. This, they argue, is vital to the transmission of "national values" and to ensure that every child is educated and safeguarded by trained professionals. This is the current view in Germany pursuant to its highest constitutional court's jurisprudence.

Advocating this latter position,[4] Emory University School of Law Professor Martha Albertson-Fineman makes the argument that it is not enough that children have the opportunity to experience a State-funded and State-controlled education; homeschooling and private schools must be banned so that all children go to public schools:

---

[3] We will not engage in a lengthy "conflict of rights" analysis that some would point to in this area. That argument goes like this: Children, as independent beings, are also endowed with rights. Therefore, if a parent makes a decision that is "in conflict" with the "child's right" then the parent's authority is illegitimate. Those who argue this also tend to argue that is the duty of the State to "supervise" parents in their role as parents and to insure that the parents carry out their "duty" properly. The United Nations Convention on the Rights of the Child (CRC) is a cornerstone for those who argue that there is conflict between parents and children in the area of rights. The CRC gives explicit instructions to treaty parties that it is their responsibility to adjudicate rights conflicts. For example, in the context of education, the CRC sets forth that children have a "right to education." See U.N. Convention on the Rights of the Child art. 28, para. 1.

[4] To be accurate, Germany does allow for private schools. However, private education in Germany must be state approved and use a state-approved curriculum. The number of private schools in Germany is relatively few in comparison to some other countries where regulations are less stringent.

The more appropriate suggestion for our current educational dilemma is that public education should be mandatory and universal. Parental expressive interest could supplement but never supplant the public institutions where the basic and fundamental lesson would be taught and experienced by all American children: we must struggle together to define ourselves both *as a collective* and as individuals.[5] (emphasis added)

University of North Carolina law professor Dr. Maxine Eichner argues that civic virtues necessary for a "liberal democracy" are not "spontaneous" and that these values must be "nurtured" in citizens through education. Not going as far down the "statist" path as Fineman, Eichner recognizes that there are different constituencies and competing interests among those who appropriately have influence and authority over children.

In a liberal democracy, it is inevitable that there will be conflicts among parents, children, and the state's interests with respect to education. Given the legitimacy of claims by the community to have a say in how its future citizens should be educated; the equally legitimate claims of parents to have a say in how their own children should be educated; the need for children to develop the autonomy that liberalism demands; and the needs of the polity to ensure that children come to possess the civic virtues necessary to perpetuate a healthy liberal democracy, none of these interests can be allowed completely to dominate education in public schools. Instead, a vigorous liberal democracy must develop a framework for education that gives all of these interests some accommodation.[6]

But Eichner is still wrong when she makes the parents' interests merely "equally legitimate" with those of the State and education. In homeschooling, these competing interests are highly visible even in the very brief history of homeschooling that this paper provides. We review this history prior to our discussion about the philosophical foundations for the diverse views in some Western democracies regarding the demarcation of the State authority and parental autonomy in education.

---

[5]   Martha Albertson-Fineman and Karen Worthington, *What is Right for Children?* (Burlington: Ashgate Publishing Company, 2009), 235.

[6]   Maxine Eichner, "Who Should Control Children's Education?: Parents, Children, and the State," (Berkley Electronic Press Legal Series, Paper 1644, 2006). http://law.bepress.com/cgi/viewcontent.cgi?article=7668&context=expresso&sei-redir=1#search="Does+the+state+have+an+interest+in+children's+education+at+all?" (accessed May 16, 2011).

Brief History of Homeschooling in America

As an attorney for the world's largest homeschool advocacy organization,[7] whose history has spanned most of the growth of the modern homeschooling movement, the author has professional awareness regarding much of the history of the movement. In the spirit of full disclosure, the author is also a homeschooling parent and thus not a disinterested observer. To argue that these views do not influence the author's conclusions would be foolish; however, he hopes that this bias does not obscure his scholarly objectivity. Those interested in a more complete history of the homeschooling movement are encouraged to consult *Homeschool: An American History* by Dr. Milton Gaither, associate professor of education at Messiah College.

Pointing to notable homeschooled heroes in history like George Washington, Abraham Lincoln, and Theodore Roosevelt; Generals George Patton and Douglas MacArthur; scientists Albert Einstein, Blaise Pascal, and Booker T. Washington; and many others, homeschool advocates assert that, historically, parents were primarily responsible for their children's education by either personally providing or arranging for it.[8] After all, it was not until the early 20th century that all American states even had laws requiring that children attend some form of State-sanctioned school. After this, parents who did not send their child to school at all could be prosecuted for truancy, a criminal offense in most states. But compulsory attendance ages were still only from about age 8 until around 14. Over the next century, however, the compulsory attendance age range would expand until today where most states have compulsory attendance ages ranging from as early as 5 to as high as 18. This is true in most Western democracies.

Lighting the Fuse

In the 1960s, two influential education researchers and practitioners in the U.S. were becoming increasingly critical of the public education system. In his books *How Children Fail*, *How Children Learn*, and *Deschooling Society*, John Holt, a Yale graduate and longtime teacher and teacher trainer,

---

[7]   HSLDA (Home School Legal Defense Association) is an U.S.-based nonprofit association with over 80,000 member families. For more information see www.hslda.org.

[8]   Bridgeway Academy, "Famous Homeschoolers," Homeschool Academy, http://www.homeschoolacademy.com/famoushomeschoolers.htm (accessed May 16, 2011).

wrote scathing condemnations of "institutional schooling."[9] Holt was a
true sixties individualist whose basic contention was that compulsory
schooling destroys a child's natural curiosity and replaces subject matter
learning with skill learning and a desire to please the teacher rather than to
explore his own interests.[10] Dr. Raymond Moore, a Seventh-day Adventist,
also published several critiques against public education in the 1960s. Then
in the mid-1970s, Moore wrote *Better Late than Early* and *Schooling Can
Wait* to argue against the current push to get children into school earlier via
early education and prekindergarten programs. The Moores had
homeschooled their own children in the 1940s and 1950s.[11] Both Holt and
Moore became strong advocates for homeschooling. Both men made important contributions to the start of this dynamic educational movement.

In 1978, Holt, considered one of the more popular educational writers
in America, appeared on the television talk show *Donahue* to discuss
homeschooling. Produced against the backdrop of increasingly famous
cases of parents being prosecuted for homeschooling, the show was among
the very first mainstream media appearances about homeschooling. The
result of this media appearance was an immediate increase in the prestige
and awareness of homeschooling.[12] A similar event happened within the
Christian community in 1979 and again in 1982 when Dr. James Dobson, a
child psychologist and former teacher who founded the evangelical ministry *Focus on the Family*, hosted Dr. Raymond Moore on a series of his
daily radio programs. Dobson's influence within the growing evangelical
community meant that thousands of parents tuned in to the 200 radio sta-
tions that then broadcast his show. Many Christian homeschooling pioneers point to Dr. Moore's appearances on Dr. Dobson's programs as the
first time they heard about the concept of homeschooling.

In retrospect, it appears that these two personalities and their respective
mainstream media appearances struck a chord with groups of parents who
were unhappy with public education in America at the time for their own
reasons. As these parents explored the idea of home education, they were,
however, immediately confronted with the realities of compulsory attendance laws. Because homeschooling was only tolerated in a handful of
states, homeschooling meant, for most parents, not only attempting a new
"untested" form of education, but also possible civil disobedience with the

---

9   Milton Gaither, *Homeschool: An American History* (New York: Palgrave Macmil-
     lan, 2008), 123.
10   Ibid.
11   Ibid., 129.
12   Ibid., 126.

potential for criminal prosecution. Today, homeschooling pioneers relay tales to newer homeschoolers about the "old days" where they had to have elaborate escape plans or procedures to hide should a truant officer or social worker appear at their door. Such pressure was untenable and homeschoolers organized in order to address the intractable legal challenges.

During the early years of the movement, few American states had any laws addressing homeschooling.[13] Thus, prior to 1980, homeschooling was largely an "illegal" undertaking with an uncertain future.[14] Earlier court rulings had not favored homeschoolers. For example, in 1929, the New Hampshire Supreme Court ruled that children tutored at home missed out on important "association with all classes of society," thus disallowing homeschooling.[15] Similar rulings are found in California in 1953[16] and Kansas in 1963.[17] One of the earliest positive cases for homeschooling, *People v. Levisen (1950)*, in Illinois was a hint of what would come later, albeit nearly 40 years later.

But even as homeschooling laws and regulations were passed by various legislative bodies in the 1980s allowing for homeschooling, increasing numbers of homeschoolers resulted in increasing conflicts between homeschooling parents and authorities. These "showdowns" ranged from tense meetings between parents and superintendents, truant officer visits to homes, social worker visits with threatened removal, and in some cases actual removal, of children from a home, to at least one documented incident of homicide where a homeschooling father's death resulted from an altercation with local law enforcement where homeschooling was one of the issues. These showdowns turned into hundreds of cases throughout the U.S. over several decades. As homeschool historian Milton Gaither notes, "local officials by the mid-1980s typically [did] not harbor goodwill toward homeschoolers . . ."[18]

---

13   Ibid., 179–199. See also Christopher J. Klicka, *Homeschooling: The Right Choice* (Gresham: Noble Publishing Associates, 1995), 380.

14   Many homeschoolers argued that they had a fundamental constitutional right under the United States Supreme Court's cases to homeschool their children. Thus, they argued, even if state laws did not explicitly provide an exception to compulsory attendance laws for homeschooling, Supreme Court case law, they argued, granted one.

15   *State v. Hoyt*, 146 A. 170 (N.H. 1929).

16   *People v. Turner* (1953) 121 Cal. App. 2d Supp. 861.

17   *State v. Lowry*, 383 P.2d 962 (Ks. 1963).

18   Gaither, 181.

Overcoming Objections

As homeschoolers organized to exert influence on their elected officials both at the state and national level, there were three primary areas of resistance that had to be overcome. The first, as observed, was the legal status of homeschooling. This will be examined in more detail later. The other major objections to the concept of homeschooling were raised in regard to academic outcomes: The second objection concerned teacher competency and the third was socialization. The teacher competency objection essentially asserted that mothers (who, in nearly all cases, did the teaching at home) were not qualified to teach their children. How, the question went, could an unqualified mother who had, in most cases, no specialized training in education or even a college degree in many cases, possibly match educational outcomes that would result from the focused attention of a college-educated, trained, and state-certified public school teacher? The third objection, socialization, was usually couched in terms of the need for children to go to school with children their own age in order to learn how to get along. This objection came with a related, although relatively infrequently raised, corollary about the lack of oversight and concomitant potential of latent physical abuse or neglect of homeschooled children who were "off the radar."[19]

Somewhat incredulous education professionals observed the burgeoning homeschooling movement with varying degrees of concern. National Education Association's Robert McClure said that "it's important for children to move outside their families and learn how to function with strangers," expressing fear that home education would undermine commitment to American pluralism.[20] Omar Norton of the Maine Department of Education stated that "instruction in isolation cannot compare with a child being educated in a group." Texas Federation of Teachers President John Cole observed that "if anyone can teach, teaching will, indeed, no longer be a profession."[21] Donald Venus, a supervisor of public instruction in Michigan, put it this way: "If you need a license to cut hair, then you should have one to mold a kid's mind."[22] Education professionals were not alone.

---

[19] "Off the radar" means that the children were not being seen outside their family on a regular basis. Therefore, argued some, there was no way for an independent set of eyes to see them and interact with them to determine whether or not they were being abused.

[20] Gaither, 181.

[21] Ibid.

[22] Ibid., 182.

When asked in a Gallup survey whether homeschooling was a good or bad thing, only 16% of the American public in 1985 said that it was good. That number rose to 41% in 2001. However, as the 16% in 1985 illustrates, not many people were enthusiastic about homeschooling in the early years.[23] Now, after 30-plus years of increasing experience, scientific research is providing strong evidence exposing the flaws in these criticisms.

Making the Grade

According to a website maintained by Dr. Robert Kunzman, professor of education at Indiana University, more than 1500 articles have been written since 1919 about homeschooling, most since 1975.[24] Dr. Kunzman's website shows that nearly 200 have been written on the academic performance of homeschooled students. Addressing the issue of academic performance, and thereby dealing with the objection of teacher competency, several researchers have surveyed tens of thousands of homeschooled students dating back to 1990. These works include a study by Dr. Brian Ray (1990), then professor at Seattle Pacific University, and Dr. Lawrence Rudman (1999), director of the ERIC clearinghouse on assessment and evaluation, and Dr. Ray again in 2000 and 2010.[25] These studies showed that homeschooled students' academic performance on standardized tests is generally as much as 25 to 35 percentile points higher than the average public school students'.[26] Critics of the studies, including Dr. Kunzman, have expressed concerns with data collection and methodology, primarily

---

[23] It does not appear that the poll question has been repeated more recently. However, it is probably not a stretch to suggest that the results of a current poll question would likely top the 50% "good" barrier.

[24] Robert Kunzman, Homeschooling Research & Scholarship, http://www.indiana.edu/~homeeduc/research_homepage.html (accessed May 17, 2011).

[25] Brian D. Ray, "Home schooling: The ameliorator of negative influences on learning?" *Peabody Journal of Education*, 75, No. 1/2 (2000): 71–106. See also Brian D. Ray, "Academic Achievement and Demographic Traits of Homeschool Students: A Nationwide Study," *Academic Leadership Journal*, 8, No. 1, (2010) http://www.academicleadership.org/emprical_research/Academic_Achievement_a nd_Demographic_Traits_of_Homeschool_Students_A_Nationwide_Study.shtml (accessed February 10, 2010). And see Lawrence M. Rudner, "Scholastic Achievement and Demographic Characteristics of Home School Students in 1998," *Educational Policy Analysis Archives*, 7, No. 8 (1999), http://epaa.asu.edu/ojs/article/viewFile/543/666 (accessed January 21, 2010).

[26] Home School Legal Defense Association and Brian Ray, "Home School Progress Report 2009: Academic Achievement and Demographics," (2009), see http://www.hslda.org/docs/study/ray2009/2009_Ray_StudyFINAL.pdf.

with respect to self-selection in the data population. Dr. Brian Ray, a long-time homeschool researcher and founder of the National Home Education Research Institute (NHERI) has analyzed several of these studies and produced reports about them. These reports can be accessed at the Home School Legal Defense Association's website (www.hslda.org/research). Interestingly, Dr. Ray's studies also found that there is no or only minimal correlation between a homeschool teacher's credentials or qualifications and the academic performance of the child. Essentially, this meant that a homeschooling mother who did not have a high school diploma and any homeschooling mother who had a Ph.D. would, on average, achieve similar results. Students taught by both were 25 to 35 percentile points higher than the national average representing public school students.

It is important to note that even severe critics of homeschooling usually acknowledge that homeschooling can be and probably is *usually* successful. In a severe critique of "unregulated homeschooling," Georgetown Professor of Law Robin West recognizes this while pointing to some of the underlying structural factors that make homeschooling successful.

> . . . although I will be criticizing the right to completely deregulated homeschooling, I do not mean to deny for a moment that homeschooling itself is often—maybe usually—successful, when done responsibly. Passionately involved and loving parents, whether religious or not, can often better educate their children in small tutorials at home, than can cash-strapped, under-motivated, inadequately supported, and overwhelmed public school teachers with too many students in their classrooms. Results bear this out, as homeschool advocates repeatedly point out (and as critics virtually never deny): the homeschooled children who are tested, or who take college boards, whether or not religious, perhaps surprisingly, perhaps not, do very well on standardized tests, and on the average, they do better than their public school counterparts.[27]

West, Eichner, and others argue that society has such an interest in regulating the education of children because these children are the future of "their" democratic society. Therefore the State should be able to significantly regulate homeschooling. They do not go quite as far as calling for its outright prohibition, like Fineman, but generally point to the need for registration, curriculum oversight, and mandatory state-sponsored testing—which, however, are not required by most American states.

---

[27]   Robin L. West, "The Harms of Homeschooling," *Philosophy & Public Policy Quarterly* 29, No. 3/4 (Summer/fall 2009): 9.

Can't We Just Get Along?

Dr. Kunzman reports that over 220 articles have been written regarding socialization of homeschooled students since 1984.[28] One 2003 study by Dr. Ray surveyed nearly 5000 homeschool graduates. In *Home Educated and Now Adults*, Dr. Ray found that homeschooled students were more civically active and participated in more extracurricular activities than the average public school student.[29] Dr. Ray's research shows that homeschooled children go to college, enter the workforce, become active in politics and are highly involved in their communities at rates equal to or higher than their peers in other educational settings. Another study performed by Dr. David J. Francis and Dr. Timothy Keefe, published in 2004, found that the social skills and competencies of homeschooled children, as measured on standardized tests, were as good as or better than those of public school children.[30] Dr. Richard Medlin offers the most recent synthesis of research on the social, emotional, and psychological development of the home educated. In his work, Dr. Medlin found that home educated students are active and well-adjusted.[31] These findings make sense when one looks below the surface to see how homeschooling works.

In homeschooling, children are not tied to a set schedule or physical brick-and-mortar location. Homeschooling is in many cases as much a lifestyle as it is a form of education. It allows for far greater flexibility for children to follow their own interests—to a much greater extent than most public school children are able to do. News reports frequently highlight homeschooled students who have made notable accomplishments in large part because they were not tied to a traditional educational setting. For example, in July 2009, homeschooled teenager Zac Sunderland became the youngest person to circumnavigate the world. Actor Will Smith and his wife Jade explained to *Essence* magazine that they homeschool their children because it allows "for flexibility so they can stay with us when we

---

[28] Kunzman, Robert, *Homeschooling Research and Scholarship Website, Topic: Socialization,* http://www.indiana.edu/~homeeduc/topic_socialization.html accessed November 15, 2011.

[29] Brian D. Ray, *Home Educated and Now Adults: Their Community and Civic Involvement, Views about Homeschooling, and Other Traits,* (Salem, OR: National Home Education Research Institute, 2004).

[30] David J. Francis and Timothy Z. Keith, "Social Skills of Homeschooled and Conventionally School Children: A Comparison Study," *The Homeschool Researcher* 16, No. 1 (2004): 15–24.

[31] Richard G. Medlin. "Homeschooled Children's Social Skills." *Home School Researcher,* 17(1) (2006): 1–8.

travel and also because the school system in this country—public and private—is designed for the industrial age. We're in the technological age. We don't want our kids to memorize. We want them to learn."[32] Homeschoolers have also won a disproportionate number of national science, math, spelling, geography, and other academic competitions.[33]

We Fought the Law and We Won

Research finding that this form of education can produce such outcomes would not have been possible if homeschoolers had been unsuccessful in their legal defense in courts and state legislatures. In the early 1980s, homeschoolers formed organizations, hired lobbyists, and attended hundreds of state and local regulatory hearings in order to exert grassroots political influence. To this day, homeschooling hearings and votes at state legislatures are the stuff of legend. In at least two recent examples, homeschoolers broke all records of public attendance at hearings in Nebraska and Illinois when their rights to homeschool were threatened.[34] State legislators and public policy officials have come to know that homeschoolers are a potentially powerful political force. This was not always the case, however.

During the early years, individuals and small groups of homeschoolers had to hire their own lawyers or depend on the goodwill (of which there was usually very little, as noted) of legislators or local school officials. In 1983, a national organization called the Home School Legal Defense Association (HSLDA) was founded. This national organization defended in-

---

[32] Gaither, 221.

[33] Brief of Amicus Curiae Home School Legal Defense Association, Christian Home Educators Of New Hampshire, and Catholics United For Home Education In Support Of Petitioner, *In The Matter Of Martin F. Kurowski, and Brenda A. Kurowski,* Supreme Court of New Hampshire (2010), (No. 2009-0751). Slip opinion at   http://www.courts.state.nh.us/supreme/opinions/2011/2011026kurowski.pdf. http://www.hslda.org/hs/state/nh/NH_Amicus_Brief_5_19_2010.pdf   (accessed May 17, 2011), 9–14.

[34] This information is from personal observation in testimony. In February 2008, I attended a hearing in Lincoln, Nebraska about LB 1141, a bill that would have imposed restrictions on homeschooling parents. Capital officials told me that the number in attendance, well over 1200 individuals, broke attendance records for a hearing at the Capitol. A similar occurrence happened in early 2011 in Springfield, Illinois. HSLDA Staff Attorney Scott Woodruff testified against SB136. Attorney Woodruff reported that according to officials in Springfield, attendance was astonishing and record-breaking.

dividual homeschoolers and influenced state and federal legislatures. This organization, along with many state and local homeschool organizations, helped to shift the power imbalance. Although many homeschoolers argued that they had a federal constitutional right to homeschool, only a handful of American states made an exception to compulsory attendance laws for homeschooling. Homeschoolers in each state had to discover an appropriate strategy as they went along.

In some states, individual families attempted to comply with the laws by forming individual private schools. Others came together to form "umbrella" private schools. In most states, stemming in part from the 1925 United States Supreme Court's landmark decision *Pierce v. Society of Sisters* and historical practice, private school laws were quite minimal.[35] However, this practice was tested in court. One of the earliest favorable homeschooling cases, as previously mentioned, was in Illinois in 1950. In *People v. Levinsen*, the Illinois courts recognized that home instruction was properly recognized under the private school law. In 1967, the New Jersey State Supreme Court reversed its earlier ruling that children could not be homeschooled and wrote that "to hold that the statute requires equivalent social contact and development would emasculate this alternative and allow only group education, thereby eliminating private tutoring for home education."[36] Overall, courts seemed to focus more on academics and minimum educational standards than socialization—although socialization was certainly an issue and continues to be in individual court cases.[37] By the 1980s, "rulings tended in the general direction of finding that homeschools do count as private schools, and that they should be only evaluated by academics, not social standards."[38] This strategy met with success. Today, 14 states, including California, Colorado, Illinois, and Texas recognize the right of parents to educate their own children under the auspices of their private school statutes.[39]

---

[35]   *Pierce v. Society of Sisters*, 268 U.S. 510 (1925).

[36]   *State v. Massa*, 95 N.J. Super. 382 (Morris County, 1967). New Jersey parents did not have to form private schools, but were simply required to provide "equivalent instruction."

[37]   See *In Matter of Martin F. Kurowski and Brenda A. Kurowski*, Case No. 2009-751 (NH S.Ct., Mar. 16, 2011).

[38]   Gaither, 180. (e.g. the academic product, child's evidence of learning rather than the process, curriculum or parental qualifications)

[39]   See *Jonathan L. v. Superior Court*, 81 Cal. Rptr. 3d 571, Cal. App. 2 Dist., 2008; *People in Interest of D.B.*, 767 P.2d 801 (Colo. App. 1988); *People v. Levisen*, 404 Ill. 574, 90 N.E.2d 213 (1950); *Leeper v. Arlington Indep. School Dist.*, No. 17-88761-85 Tarrant County 17th Judicial Ct. Apr. 13, 1987). See also Christopher J.

However, for parents in states without amenable private school statutes, other solutions were required. In these states, conflicts arose over the implementation or interpretation of statutes and regulations. One way homeschoolers often challenged laws was to allege that a law or regulation was unconstitutionally vague—meaning that a reasonable person could not reasonably understand how to interpret the law. Another tactic was for homeschoolers to assert that a law or regulation violated parents' fundamental federal and/or state constitutional rights. Homeschoolers would argue that laws interfered with their fundamental constitutional rights to direct their child's education or unreasonably infringed upon their religious convictions. However, the United States Supreme Court's decision in *Pierce* recognized that parents had a federally protected constitutional right to direct the education and upbringing of their children.

> The fundamental theory of liberty upon which all governments of this Union repose exclude any general power of the state to standardize its children by forcing them to accept teaching from public teachers only. The child is not the ***mere creature of the state***; those who nurture him and direct his destiny have the right, coupled with the high duty, to recognize and prepare him for additional obligations.[40] (emphasis added)

Some parents argued that their federal constitutional First Amendment right to freedom of religious expression was violated by laws that were too restrictive. These laws clashed with parents' religious convictions that parents were responsible to God for the education of their children and any state regulation interfered with that right by interfering with the parents' and children's relationship with God.

In some states, certain qualifications were required for parents such as teacher certification or possessing a high school diploma. In West Virginia, for example, the law required that a homeschooling parent have at least four years more education than the grade level of the child they were teaching. This requirement was altered by the legislature in 2005 after which only a high school diploma was required. Until 1993, Michigan required all teachers to be certified by the state. Teacher qualifications were a common requirement in the early days of the homeschooling movement. Today,

---

Klicka, *Untangling The Red Tape: The Details You Need To Homeschool in the 50 States* (Purcellville: HSLDA, 2009), iv.
[40]   *Pierce v. Society of Sisters*, 268 U.S. 510.

however, only eight states require parents to have either a high school diploma or a GED.[41]

State courts usually found ways to rule in favor of homeschoolers without addressing the religious freedom arguments.[42] However, one of the most significant victories for homeschoolers came in Michigan on this very claim. In *People v. DeJonge*, the Michigan Supreme Court ruled that it was an unconstitutional infringement on religious expression to require teacher certification for parents who homeschool their children for religious reasons. In that case, the Michigan Supreme Court declared:

> In summary, we conclude that the historical underpinnings of the First Amendment to the U.S. Constitution and the case law in support of it compels the conclusion that the imposition of the certification requirement upon the DeJonges violates the Free Exercise Clause. We so conclude because we find that the certification requirement is not essential to nor is it the least restrictive means of achieving the State's claimed interest. Thus, we reaffirm that sphere of inviolable conscience and belief which is the mark of a free people. [. . .] We hold that the teacher certification requirement is an unconstitutional violation of the Free Exercise Clause of the First Amendment as applied to families whose religious convictions prohibit the use of certified teachers. Such families, therefore, are exempt from the dictates of the teacher certification requirements.[43] (internal citation removed)

As of 1993, homeschooling had become legal and increasingly popular in every state in the United States. Victories came at great effort and expense, but homeschoolers were greatly helped by American cultural values which respect pluralism, individuality, and religious freedom. Initially, there were only a few states where American homeschoolers could safely

---

[41] Christopher J. Klicka, *Untangling the Red Tape*, v. GED means general equivalency diploma. The GED is an equivalent to a high school diploma issued to a student who takes and passes a state-approved test. It is beyond the scope of this paper to look at the regulatory regimes off all 50 states, HSLDA has created a four-level framework to analyze state regulations depending upon four key attributes of state laws. Every state is ranked according to whether they require notice, evaluation of student progress, teacher credentials, approval by public officials, or home visits. This analysis may be found at www.HSLDA.org/laws. GED means general equivalency diploma. The GED is an equivalent to a high school diploma issued to a student who takes and passes a state-approved test.

[42] Gaither, 179.

[43] Christopher J. Klicka, *The Right to Homeschool: A Guide to the Law on Parents' Rights in Education* 3d ed., (Durham: Carolina Academic Press, 1995), 66–67 quoting *People v. DeJonge*, 501 N.W.2d 127, 144 (Mich. 1993).

homeschool. The fact that there were other states that had explicit provisions for homeschooling was a good legal argument for homeschooling. Such a fact also provided evidence that homeschooling existed as a legitimate and legally recognized form of education. Because other states had experience with homeschooling, a favorable context existed for judges and legislatures in other states to evaluate homeschooling and make their own determination about whether and how to provide for it in their law.

Demarcation

We turn now to analyze various educational philosophies and frameworks that originate in large part from European thinkers. As we do, we see a similar picture beginning to emerge. Cultures grappling with increasingly ineffective public education systems find some parents seeking alternatives. Homeschooling is among them. And as parents seek to explore homeschooling, they are finding resistance based in the philosophies we will discuss. These parents are few in number—like American homeschoolers during the early days. They are seeking to change the minds of public policy makers and public opinion. However, they do not have the same cultural traditions or experience as in America or other English-speaking societies where homeschooling has flourished with relative ease. By understanding the historical roots of these philosophies the author hopes that policymakers will be able to think critically about their response to homeschooling.

In their three-volume work, *Balancing Freedom, Autonomy, and Accountability in Education*, Dr. Charles Glenn and Dr. Jan de Groof agree with the United States Supreme Court's decision in *Pierce* that the right of parents to guide the development of their children and to choose the appropriate form of education for them is *fundamental.* They write that "to deny that choice . . . is unjust and unworthy of a free society."[44] They also remind their readers that the fundamental right of parents to educational freedom is recognized internationally.[45] A review of several foundational human rights documents shows that the right of parents to control and direct their children's education is a tenet of human rights doctrine and is not only recognized, but is also superior in relation to the claims of the State in educating children.

---

[44] Charles Glenn and Jan De Groof, *Balancing Freedom, Autonomy and Accountability in Education*, (Nijmegen, Netherlands: Wolf Legal Publishers, 2005), 1.

[45] Ibid, 6.

Article 26, part 3, of *The Universal Declaration of Human Rights of 1948* states that "parents have a *prior right* to choose the kind of education that shall be given to their children" (emphasis added). The fact that the word "prior" is used is indicative of the hierarchy and primacy of the right of parents in relation to the State. The 1950 *European Convention for the Protection of Human Rights and Fundamental Freedoms* provides in Article 2 that,

> in the exercise of any functions which it assumes in relation to education and teaching, the State shall respect the right of parents to ensure such education and teaching in conformity with their own religious and philosophical convictions.

In 1966, the United Nations General Assembly opened the *International Covenant on Economic, Social and Cultural Rights* for signature. The covenant entered into force in 1976. Article 13.3 states:

> The States Parties to the present covenant undertake to have respect for the liberty of parents [. . .] to choose for their children schools, other than those established by public authorities, which conform to such minimum educational standards as may be laid down or approved by the State and to ensure that religious or moral education of their children is in conformity with their own convictions.

Even though this covenant allows the State to create certain "minimum educational standards," it reaffirms the *Human Rights Declaration's* recognition of parents' rights. That same year, 1976, the *International Covenant on Civil and Political Rights* went into effect, providing in Article 18, paragraph 4 that:

> The States Parties to the present Covenant undertake to have respect for the liberty of parents and, when applicable, legal guardians to ensure the religious and moral education of their children in conformity with their own convictions.

Without quibbling over or parsing what it means to "ensure . . . education in conformity with their own convictions," it seems eminently clear, *as a foundational principle,* that the right of parents to direct their children's education is considered a human right that must be respected by states professing an allegiance to the human rights set forth in these documents.

Why is it, then, as Glenn and de Groof write, that the concept of educational freedom today enjoys "far less support" from progressive elites "than do other human rights, such as the freedoms of speech, the press, religious belief, and voluntary association"?[46] Why is it that progressive elites "see family as a source of resistance to social progress and put their trust in government-sponsored schooling to make children more progressive and more enlightened than their parents"? [47] Why then, are there countries like Germany, Sweden, Brazil, the Canadian province of Quebec, and others that claim to respect human rights norms, yet ban, actually or effectively, homeschooling, or persecute parents who engage in it? Why is it that the education of a child is so controversial? Why is there such a struggle between parents and governments over how, what, when, and where a child learns?

To answer these questions, we will observe philosophically how several countries, including the United States, Canada, England, France, and Germany, have addressed and now address the issue of parental authority versus State authority in education. We commence with the American experience, beginning with the initiation of compulsory attendance laws and the eventual takeover of public education by the humanist movement. This takeover contributed significantly to conflicts between parents and government schools over values, which, as much as methodology and lackluster performance, led to widespread dissatisfaction, thereby helping to create a fertile environment for the homeschooling movement in America.

United States of America

In 1979, the United States Supreme Court in *Parham v. J.R.* articulated the enduring philosophy of American jurisprudence with respect to parental autonomy when it wrote that "fit parents are deemed to act in the best interests of their children."[48] Absent behavior to the contrary, parents are free to make decisions about and for their children without government intrusion or oversight. The Court wrote eloquently:

> Our jurisprudence historically has reflected Western civilization concepts of the family as a unit with broad parental authority over minor children. Our cases have consistently followed that course; our constitutional system long ago rejected any notion that a child is "the mere creature of the State" and, on the contrary, asserted that parents generally "have the right, coupled with the high duty, to recognize and prepare [their children] for additional

---

[46] Ibid., 7.
[47] Ibid.
[48] *Parham v. J.R.* 442 U.S. 584, 600 (1979).

obligations" . . . Surely, this includes a "high duty" to recognize symptoms of illness and to seek and follow medical advice. The law's concept of the family rests on a presumption that parents possess what a child lacks in maturity, experience, and capacity for judgment required for making life's difficult decisions. More important, historically it has recognized that natural bonds of affection lead parents to act in the best interests of their children.[49] (internal citations omitted)

Yet the legal future of homeschooling—in many ways a reaction to what was happening in America's public schools at that time—remained in doubt. This was true despite the Court's assurances that parental autonomy in education was an enduring tradition of Western civilization. By 1979, public schools in America had become, by judicial order, explicitly and exclusively secular. This, however, was not the case for the first one hundred years or so of public education in America—nor was it the vision of a primary founder, Horace Mann.

Mann served as the first commissioner of education in Massachusetts (the first in the country), where compulsory education was first legislated in 1642. He believed that religion and morality were indispensible in the public schools, where he envisioned national unity would be forged by shared national values and fostered through common education.

> Directly and indirectly, the influences of the Board of Education have been the means of increasing, to a great extent, the amount of religious instruction given in our schools. Moral training, or the application of religious principles to the duties of life, should be its inseparable accompaniment. No community can long subsist, unless it has religious principle as the foundation of moral action; nor unless it has moral action as the super structure of religious principle.[50]

But in 1947, just a century after Mann pioneered compulsory attendance in Massachusetts, the United States Supreme Court wrote that in public education the government must observe a "wall of separation between church

---

[49] *Parham v. J.R.,* Internal citations: *Pierce v. Society of Sisters,* 268 U.S. 510, 268 U.S. 535 (1925). See also *Wisconsin v. Yoder,* 406 U.S. 205, 406 U.S. 213 (1972); *Prince v. Massachusetts,* 321 U.S. 158, 321 U.S. 166 (1944); *Meyer v. Nebraska,* 262 U.S. 390, 262 U.S. 400 (1923), 1 W. Blackstone, Commentaries *447; 2 J. Kent, Commentaries on American Law *190

[50] *Ninth Annual Report of the Secretary of the Board* (Boston: Dutton & Wentworth, 1846), 157.

and state."[51] Over the next 30 years, an active federal judiciary would utterly dismantle Mann's vision of a religion-based morality in the public schools. Key rulings include prayer being unconstitutional in public schools,[52] the elimination of Bible reading,[53] and the prohibition of teaching theories of creation science or intelligent design in addition to the theory of evolution.[54]

Glenn writes that Mann may have missed the controversy his vision would later provoke:

> Apparently Mann could not see that, for some of his opponents, the confidence in human goodness and improvability that he wished the common school to teach represented a false doctrine, corrosive of the basis of their faith.[55]

Initially, the controversy Glenn refers to was *between* religious denominations. Most parents objected to the nonsectarian religious instruction Mann contemplated. They wanted their children to receive doctrinal instruction in their own religion. Ultimately it would not be those who disagreed with Mann's *religious doctrine*, but rather those who disagreed with the inclusion of *any religion at all* in schools who would dismantle Mann's vision and impose a form of secular humanism in the public schools, thereby effectively replacing Mann's religion-based morality. This replacement of Mann's religion-based morality with a religion of secular humanism,[56] which has as one of its primary objectives the liberation of humanity from antiquated and superstitious notions about God and religion, would become an important ingredient in the disaffection between many parents and public schools. This became a leading factor in the initiation and growth of the American homeschooling movement beginning in the 1980s.

Leading proponents of secular humanism saw the public school system as a natural building block in the establishment of their worldview and their vision for future American society. Charles Francis Potter, founder of

---

[51] *Everson v. Board of Education*, 330 U.S. 1 (1947), 16, citing *Reynolds v. United States*, 98 U.S. 145, 164.

[52] *Engel v. Vitale*, 370 U.S. 421 (1962).

[53] *School Dist. of Abington TP. v. Schempp*, 374 U.S. 203 (1963).

[54] *Mozert v. Hawkins City Board of Education* 827 F.2d 1058 (1987)

[55] Glenn, 169.

[56] In footnote 11 in *Torcaso v. Watkins*, 367 U.S. 488 (1961), the United States Supreme Court noted that Secular Humanism is a religion. See also discussion, "Is Secular Humanism Religion", http://vftonline.org/Patriarchy/definitions/humanism_religion.htm (accessed May 24, 2011).

the First Humanist Society of New York, wrote and signed the Humanist Manifesto along with others, such as his contemporary and influential architect of the modern American public school system, John Dewey. Potter, in 1930, wrote:

> Education is thus our most powerful ally of humanism, and every public school is a school of humanism. What can the theistic Sunday school, meeting for an hour once a week, and teaching only a fraction of the children, do to stem the tide of a five-day program of humanistic teachings?[57]

Harvard Professor of Education Chester Pierce reaffirmed this vision for public education 40 years later:

> Every child in America entering school at the age of five is mentally ill because he comes to school with certain allegiances to our Founding Fathers, toward our elected officials, toward his parents, toward a belief in a supernatural being, and toward the sovereignty of this nation as a separate entity. It's up to you as teachers to make all these sick children well—by creating the international child of the future.[58]

To be sure, many homeschooling families have held and do hold that religion has nothing to do with their decision to homeschool, but the above-expressed hostility toward religious instruction and traditional values—which most parents deemed important, if not essential in the education of their children—caused many religious parents to look for alternatives.

Interestingly, for those parents to whom religion is important, religious considerations are in many cases not the only, or even the most important factor in their decision to homeschool. In 2008, the National Center for Education Statistics released a report showing that the most important reason parents chose to homeschool was a "concern for the environment."

Many who have attempted to study the homeschooling movement have come to understand its diversity both in motivation and method. Homeschoolers have many reasons for wanting to homeschool. Some stress their desire for strong family relationships. Other researchers, like Michael Apple, Robert Reich, and Chris Lubienski, see homeschooling as

---

[57]   harles F. Potter, "Humanism: A New Religion," (New York: Simon and Schuster, 1930).

[58]   John Taylor Gatto, *The Underground History of American Education* (New York: Oxford Village Press, 2000), Chap. 13 "Bending the Student to Reality," quoting Chester M. Pierce, presented at the Childhood International Education Seminar, Boulder, Colorado, 1973;

an extreme form of the "secession of the successful" from engagement with public life.59 Others attempt to describe homeschooling as either antifeminist modernism or purely antimodernist. Some say it is libertarian or simply escapism. While in other countries religion may not be as important or a prevailing motivation to homeschool, in the United States it has been a leading factor contributing to the rapid growth of the movement.

European Influence: England, France, Germany, and Canada

In Europe, we must go back to earlier times to study the thinkers who influenced the views on the relationship between family and State. Enlightenment philosophers John Locke and Jean-Jacques Rousseau were both social contract theory philosophers whose contributions echo in political institutions today—not just in Europe but throughout the world. Locke's theories of limited government and separation of powers were integral inputs into the American Declaration of Independence of 1776 and the U.S. Constitution of 1789. Rousseau heavily influenced the bloody revolution which would move France from monarchy to republic. Yet despite their common reliance on the notion of a social contract, their views on the role of the State in educating children were quite different. The manifestation of their opposing views can be seen in national educational frameworks and cultural dynamics around the globe.

Locke's view was that nature "grants instruction solely to parental power, not to civil government."[60] In England today, the law regarding education is quite Lockean. Section 7 of the Education Act of 1996, which applies to England and Wales, states that:

> The parent of every child of compulsory school age shall cause him to receive efficient full-time education suitable—to his age, ability and aptitude, and to any special educational needs he may have, either by regular attendance at school *or otherwise*. (emphasis added)

The "or otherwise" qualification allows for private education including homeschooling. England's law is among the least restrictive homeschooling laws in the world. English authorities recognize their own limitations in official guidance to local education authorities:

---

[59]   Gaither, 225
[60]   Tarcov, 5.

Local authorities should keep a record of children who are known to be educated at home by parents. Parents are not, however, required to inform the local authority if they decide to home educate a child who has not previously attended school.[61]

Rousseau, on the other hand, viewed the State as the supreme authority with respect to children. He firmly understood the importance of education and its role in shaping society. It was necessary, he thought, to compel parents to give up their children to receive an education that reflected the enlightenment values of the impending French Revolution. The State, in Rousseau's world, must control education.

> From the first moment of life, men ought to begin learning to deserve to live; and, as at the instant of birth we partake of the rights of citizenship, that instant ought to be the beginning of the exercise of our duty. If there are laws for the age of maturity, there ought to be laws for infancy, teaching obedience to others: and as the reason of each man is not left to be the sole arbiter of his duties, government ought the less indiscriminately to abandon to the intelligence and prejudices of fathers the education of their children, as that education is of still greater importance to the State than to the fathers: for, according to the course of nature, the death of the father often deprives him of the final fruits of education; but his country sooner or later perceives its effects. Families dissolve but the State remains.[62]

For Rousseau, the State was the stabilizing force in society and thus had to take control of the education of children in order to enable them—and the State—to fulfill their ultimate potential. Revolutionaries maintained that parents would have to give way in order for France to discard the monarchy for republican values. One revolutionary official at that time wrote to colleagues in Paris:

> Citizen Minister . . . don't expect anything without regenerative violence, since the stubbornness of parents is such that it can only be overcome by conquering it.[63]

---

[61]   2009 Statutory Guidance on Children at Risk of Not Receiving Suitable Education, http://www.education-otherwise.org/cme.htm (accessed May 17, 2011).

[62]   Jean Jacques Rousseau, *A Discourse on Political Economy* and *Considerations for the Government of Poland*, (1755), 148–149. See also Charles Leslie Glenn, Jr., *The Myth of the Common School* (Amherst: University of Massachusetts Press, 1988), 18.

[63]   Glenn, 29.

France has made significant progress from the days of the revolution with respect to home education. France does not ban homeschooling but does heavily regulate the practice. Regional officers assigned by the national education ministry annually inspect homeschooling families, who must also register annually with their local political authority. In France, there are estimated to be just a few thousand homeschooled students, whereas in the United Kingdom there are tens of thousands.

It is interesting to observe that in Canada these two philosophies express themselves in one modern nation-state. In English-speaking Canada, home education legal requirements are minimal, whereas in more heavily French-influenced and French-speaking Québec, homeschooling laws are far more restrictive and homeschooling is viewed with greater suspicion. A review of the website of the Association of Parent-Educators of Québec shows that while homeschooling is legal in Québec, there has been great controversy over the practice. Québec's education law states that a compulsory school exemption applies to "a student who receives homeschooling and benefits from an educational experience which, according to an evaluation made by or for the school board, are equivalent to what is provided at school."[64] The controversies appear to be the different interpretations of the various school boards in Québec as well as the different interpretation of the ministry of education in Québec regarding the mechanics of evaluation which the law makes allowance for.

Advocates for homeschoolers in Québec argue that the *Canadian Charter of Rights and Freedoms* requires that parents be provided with options to satisfy the evaluation requirement.[65] These advocates further complain that the local authorities have attempted to require the use of particular curriculum as well as to force the use of a particular evaluation methodology. Advocates for homeschoolers also complain that local authorities are quick to involve the protective services organization against homeschooling families. Thus, while homeschooling is legal in Québec, there is conflict between local and central authorities and homeschoolers.[66]

---

[64]   R.S.Q., chapter I-13.3-15(4). See http://www2.publicationsduquebec.gouv.qc.ca/
        dynamicSearch/telecharge.php?type=2&file=/I_13_3/I13_3_A.html   (accessed
        June 9, 2011).

[65]   Canadian Charter of Rights and Freedoms, Part I of the Constitution Act, 1982,
        http://laws-lois.justice.gc.ca/eng/charter/ (accessed June 9, 2011).

[66]   For more information, see Association of Christian parent-educators of Québec,
        Legal Aspect, at http://www.acpeq.org/en/legal_aspect.html, which describes a
        decade-long series of controversies and conflicts between homeschoolers and educational authorities in Québec.

For Germany, Rousseau had some impact on educational philosophy. However, it was Prussian uniformity and bureaucracy that brought efficient public education systems to a unified Germany where, until 1938, private education and home education were generally permitted. In 1938, however, Germany outlawed private education of all forms (including homeschooling), making it a crime not to send children to school. Demonstrating the eerie philosophy that motivated the National Socialist party, the rewritten and uniform introduction to the manual for high school instructors in Germany read:

The German school is a part of the National Socialist Educational order. It is its obligation to form the national socialistic personality in cooperation with the other educational powers of the nation, but by its distinctive educational means.[67]

The dictator's vision for Europe was grotesque, but his mechanism to gain control of the German people through education illustrates the role education plays in the quest for cultural dominion. Hitler understood this when he said that the "youth of today are the people of tomorrow."[68] He further demonstrated hostility towards parental involvement in educating children when he stated:

When an opponent declares, "I will not come over to your side," I calmly say, "your child belongs to us already . . . What are you? You will pass on. Your descendents, however, now stand in the new camp. In a short time they will know nothing else but this new community."[69]

Any government that seeks to control the education of children contrary to parental direction seeks the same kind of cultural and political domination and perpetuates the same kind of offense. Incredibly, faint echoes of these ideas remain in Germany where public policy makers and judges stubbornly refuse to permit parents to homeschool their children.

In 2003, the German court system reviewed a case of a German family who wished to homeschool their children. The family was denied an exception to the compulsory school law by local education authorities and received a civil fine. The family appealed the fine to the German Constitu-

---

[67]   The Nizkor Project, *Nazi Conspiracy & Aggression*, Volume I, Chapter VII, Means Used by the Nazi Conspirators in Gaining Control of the German State (Part 44 of 55) A(1), http://www.nizkor.org/hweb/imt/nca/nca-01/nca-01-07-means-44.html (accessed May 13, 2011).

[68]   Ibid.

[69]   Adolf Hitler, quoted in William L. Shirer, *The Rise and Fall of The Third Reich* (New York: Simon and Schuster, 1960), 343.

tional Court, which upon review wrote that the "general public has a justi-fied interest in counteracting the development of religiously or philosophi-cally motivated 'parallel societies' and in integrating minorities in this area."[70] Despite the assertion to the contrary in the United Nations' *Universal Declaration of Human Rights*, the German court said that parents do not have a prior right, but rather share an equal claim with the State in the education of children:

> Social confidence in dealing with people who have different opinions, lived tolerance, the ability to assert oneself and the assertion of a conviction that differs from that of a majority opinion can be practiced more effectively if context was society and with the various views represented in society do not take place only occasionally, but rather are part of the everyday experience associated with regular school attendance.[71]

This is frightening language from a country with Germany's powerful edu-cational history, particularly at university level. What is perhaps just as frightening is the result of an appeal to the European Court of Human Rights in 2006. The Court denied the family's application stating that Germany was within its "margin of appreciation" to ban homeschooling. In reviewing the case, the Court noted that the German position—that the State had an interest *equal* to the parents in the education of children—was not a problem. The Court stated that such an outcome was "justified under Article 8 § 2 and Article 9 § 2 respectively as being provided for by law and necessary in a democratic society and in the public interest of securing the education of the child."[72] Therefore, the court found that the Konrads' application was "manifestly ill-founded." In light of explicit treaty lan-guage, including and especially the 1948 *UN Declaration of Human Rights,* this author finds the *Court's ruling* to be manifestly ill-founded!

So, apparently, did a United States federal immigration judge.

In January 2010, United States Federal Immigration Judge Lawrence O. Burman granted political asylum to a family from Germany on the basis that they were persecuted because they were members of a particular social group—homeschoolers. Judge Burman is reported to have stated:

---

[70]   Ibid.

[71]   *In the case relating to the constitutional complaint of Mr. Konrad,* German Fed-eral Constitutional Court (1 BvR 436/03, decided April 29, 2003).

[72]   European Court of Human Rights, application no. 35504/03, October 2006, by Fritz Konrad and Others against Germany, 9.

Homeschoolers are a particular social group that the German government is trying to suppress. This family has a well-founded fear of persecution . . . therefore, they are eligible for asylum . . . and the court will grant asylum.[73]

Attorneys for the family released a press document stating the following:

In his ruling, Burman said that the scariest thing about this case was the motivation of the government. He noted it appeared that rather than being concerned about the welfare of the children, the government was trying to stamp out parallel societies—something the judge called "odd" and just plain "silly." In his order the judge expressed concern that while Germany is a democratic country and is an ally, he noted that this particular policy of persecuting homeschoolers is "repellent to everything we believe as Americans."[74]

Conclusion

This paper has shown examples of the possible outcomes when governments treat children as "mere creature(s) of the state." When the State imposes its authority to override the decisions of its parent-citizens regarding their choice of education for their children, conflict follows. We have also seen that the philosophy that the State has an equal or superior claim to the education of children stands in stark contrast with modern international human rights norms as articulated by landmark human rights conventions. These international human rights documents affirm the *prior right* of parents to determine the nature of their children's education. Thus, when a court in a Western democracy, like Germany, rules as it did in its *Konrad* decision in 2003 that the State has an *equal* claim to the education of children, it demonstrates that it is operating outside the norm of internationally established human rights.

It is more than ironic that the German Constitutional Court, along with Fineman, Eichmann, Ross, and others, argues that pluralism requires the State to exercise a form of totalitarianism in education. They argue that it is the State's responsibility to ensure the existence and continuation of the free society, for which certain values (as defined by them and the State) are

---

[73] Home School Legal Defense Association, "Homeschooling Family Granted Political Asylum: Immigration Judge Says Germany Violating Basic Human Rights" (January 26, 2010), http://www.hslda.org/hs/international/Germany/201001260. asp (accessed May 16, 2011).

[74] Ibid.

necessary. Eichmann says that such "values" are not "spontaneous." Thus, the State must ensure that these values are "nurtured" through compulsory government-directed education. Those who argue in this fashion, however, conflate "society" with "State." State and society are not necessarily—and, in fact, are not usually—synonymous. Indeed, a government's interest in expanding its power may very well be at odds with the people's interest in freedom.

While Eichmann's assertion that children are not born with fully developed values and beliefs about what is necessary for a free society may be true, the absence of an inherent understanding of the values of a free society on the part of children is surely *not* a justification for compelling citizens to subject themselves or their children to compulsory government-directed education. If such a proposition were true, America would not exist today. The values that made America a free society emerged within the families that made up society at the time—mostly Christian families whose education was *not* State-controlled. Homeschooling was the prevailing form of education at the time of America's founding. The values that promote a free society certainly can emerge and be sustained regardless of whether children are taught in a public school, private school, or homeschool.

America, with a long and robust experience with homeschooling, has shown that homeschooling can deliver superior academic results and that children who are homeschooled are not only well socialized, but are also more civically minded than their peers in other educational settings. Homeschooled children are demonstrably productive and contributing members of a free, pluralistic society. In a pluralistic society, individuals *must* be permitted to hold different value systems. To argue otherwise is to argue against the fundamental understanding of pluralism and to favor totalitarianism. In Germany and France, we have seen examples of how education can be used by the State for political purposes to reshape society in accordance with the values of those in power—with catastrophic outcomes. Even today in Germany, parents are prevented from exercising their prior right, as envisioned in the *UN Declaration on Human Rights*, to choose the kind of education their children should receive.

In America, the story is somewhat different. Even though the Supreme Court recognized, as early as 1925 and subsequently in 1979 in *Parham v. J.R.*, that it was an enduring tradition of Western culture that parents have a fundamental right to direct their children's education and make decisions about their care, custody, and control, there were many conflicts during the early homeschool movement. The conflicts in the legislatures and courts in every state, which lasted over the better part of two decades, were dramatic and far-reaching. These conflicts—really the operational processes of democracy in action—resulted in a patchwork of regulatory schemes that represented diverse views as to the role between the State and education; *but* (note well) *all of them made it possible for parents to homeschool their children.* The spirit of the *UN Declaration on Human Rights* was alive and well as parents, the public, and policy makers grappled with the issue of determining the proper demarcation and authority between parents and the State in the education of children. The American experience illustrates how a Western democracy can grapple with differing points of view and develop a diverse set of regulatory schemes across its geo-political subdivisions. There is no reason to think that this could not happen elsewhere. Indeed, it should—for this is the essence of democracy in a free pluralistic society. Yet, even as such a process unfolds, it *must* be regarded as *foundational* that parents have a prior and superior right to the State regarding the education of their children.

The State *must*, if it is to be faithful to international human rights norms, recognize and protect this right, which includes the right of parents to choose to educate their children at home under their direction. This is not to say that the State may not legitimately serve in some regulatory or even oversight capacity. But to eliminate entirely the parental freedom to educate demonstrates a callous and totalitarian attitude that does not conform to modern international human rights doctrine, representing, as it surely does, the ideals of free society. Mao Tse-Tung was right when he said that "power comes from the end of a gun."[75] The State has the power to compel its citizens to conform to its laws—including compelling children to attend a government school—but to prevent or severely restrict parents from choosing how a child shall be educated (as, for example, through homeschooling) must be regarded as "unjust and unworthy of a free society."[76]

---

[75] Mao Tse-Tung, *The Little Red Book*, (Beijing, China, 1964), Chapter 5.
[76] Charles Glenn and Jan De Groof, 1.

Compulsory Education—in Schools Only?

Divergent Developments in Germany

by Thomas Schirrmacher

"Neither a government nor a party can take away the right of parents to choose an alternative form of education for their children. This is found in human rights declarations."[77]

Kristin Clemet, Minister of Education, Norway

Summary

Germany is the focus of this paper, owing to the fact that since 1938 it has had the strictest laws on compulsory schooling worldwide. The result is that homeschooling in Germany has become virtually impossible.

There are interesting divergences between policy and practice in the German setting. The *Länder* (federal states) have the responsibility for education, and they are taking a much stricter line against homeschoolers than a decade ago, especially by depriving parents of the custody of their homeschooled children at an early stage. The laws relied upon, however, were never intended to deal with such educational matters; they were designed to punish parents who abuse or neglect their children. The present, highly questionable legal action succeeds only because of the consent of state schools, state social welfare offices, and courts. The same laws are not used against the parents of the approximately 250,000 teens who are truant.

At the same time, the number of specialists in law and education (university professors in particular), as well as politicians and governmental experts who argue in favor of homeschooling—at least in specific situations like highly gifted, handicapped children, children with ADHD or for religious reasons—is growing, and the media reports on homeschooling are much more positive than they were a decade ago.

---

[77] Quote under the photo of the Minister of Education: Tor Weibye, "Ingen regjering kan fjerne foreldreretten," *Dagen* (Bergen, Norway), March 15, 2005. http://www.dagen.no/show_art.cgi?art=7299 (accessed July 2011).

This presentation will discuss in particular the functioning of the legal and sociological machinery in Germany being employed aggressively to stamp out homeschooling, while at the same time it ignores the crucial issue of parents who allow their children to skip school—thus depriving them of an adequate education at home or elsewhere. The subject will be treated against the background of Germany's educational history and present educational problems, especially as created by the high number of Muslim immigrants who never finish school.

Introduction

Compulsory schooling presents "by far the most comprehensive and most intensive invasion by the state in the personal, private sphere in the entirety of its citizens."[78] For this reason, one could expect that this happens with great caution, in a considered manner, and for the given situation only after thorough investigation. However, many are no longer at all consciously aware of what an invasion in the life of a family takes place at this point. If this invasion is desired, then it is naturally not a problem. However, if it is rejected or basically placed into question, the State cannot simply act as if it were sending demands for payments of fines to traffic offenders.

Although legal in most states in the western world, conducting homeschooling in the Federal Republic of Germany has been practically impossible to date. While in all countries neighboring Germany there are families found who are either tolerated or permitted by the authorities to instruct their children at home, in Germany this occurs illegally, in a few cases undetected, or through continuous confrontation with the authorities and courts.

The head of the Institute of Educational Research at the University of Oslo, Professor of Education Christian W. Beck, sees the increasing prevalence of homeschooling in Europe as an automatic consequence of globalization.[79] Many homeschooling parents have spent time abroad, have mar-

---

[78] Thomas Oppermann, *Kulturverwaltungsrecht* (Tübingen: Mohr, 1969), 191. See also Eggert Winter, who quotes approvingly in "Schulpflicht und Schulzwang: Überlegungen zur Strafwürdigkeit der Verletzung der Schulbesuchspflicht," *Recht der Jugend und des Bildungswesens* 26 (1978), 411.

[79] Christian W. Beck, "Home Education—Globalisation Otherwise?" Paper presented at the British Educational Research Association conference in Manchester, UK, September 15–18, 2004, http://folk.uio.no/cbeck/Home%20Education%20globalisation%202.htm. Compare also: Beck, "Home Schooling and Future Education in Norway," *European Education* 34, no. 2 (2002), 26–36 and Beck and Marta Straume, *Hjemmeundervisning–starten på en ny utdanningsrevolusjon?*

ried foreigners, grew up overseas, or regularly read foreign language literature. The internet also does its part. For these reasons, according to Beck, all European countries with the exception of Germany have become attuned to homeschooling. Instead of prohibitions, there are clear rules so State oversight remains ensured.

Nevertheless, the number of voices in Germany calling for the approval of homeschooling as an alternative to the institutionalized form of schooling in State or private schools has recently been growing.

In 2006, I published my research paper on homeschooling in Germany, written for the department of education of the University of Bonn.[80] At that time, the two editors were still not in favor of homeschooling. Both have changed their minds and argue in favor of a State-controlled homeschooling, especially for students that do not fit normal classroom education, e.g. the highly gifted or those with ADHD.

Also, since 2006, more academic studies in favor of homeschooling have been published in German than in all the preceding years combined.

Sociologist and educational scientist Ralph Fischer of Bonn, who for years has observed the setting for homeschooling in Germany, has submitted a comprehensive portrait of homeschooling in Germany from historical sources and from the present. The work introduces comprehensively supportive facilities such as distance learning schools and advocacy groups, and it traces the national and international historical development of schooling at home. In addition to that, examples of theoretical approaches on education at home from the last 200 years were cataloged, whereby important thinkers such as the educationists Johann Friedrich Herbart and Berthold Otto, the theologian and Danish national poet Nikolai Grundtvig, or the essayist Hans Magnus Enzensberger have a chance to speak and are subjected to critique from the point of view of educational science.[81]

Fischer's doctoral supervisor, Bonn Professor for Educational Science Volker Ladenthin, has assembled assessments and contributions in the pub-

---

(Oslo/Vallset: Opplandske Bokforlag, 2004). For further publications by Beck on the topic, see http://folk.uio.no/cbeck/Untitled1.htm and http://folk.uio.no/cbeck/OTHhjemmeside.htm.

[80] Thomas Schirrmacher, "Bildungspflicht statt Schulzwang," quoted in Ralph Fischer and Volker Ladenthin (eds.), *Homeschooling—Tradition und Perspektive* (Ergon: Würzburg, 2006), 199–284; also published in book form as *Bildungspflicht statt Schulzwang: Staatsrecht und Elternrecht angesichts der Diskussion um den Hausunterricht* (Bonn: VKW & Nürnberg: VTR, 2006).

[81] Ralph Fischer, *Homeschooling in der Bundesrepublik Deutschland: Eine erziehungswissenschaftliche Annäherung. Pädagogik in Europa in Geschichte und Gegenwart 1* (Bonn: VKW, 2009).

lic media in a collected volume[82] in which he advocates homeschooling and discusses reasonable ways for the State to oversee homeschooling.

After comprehensive studies on homeschooling in Switzerland, Hanniel Strebel, an economist and theologian, has put forth an educational and theological justification for homeschooling in Switzerland.[83]

In a 2009 report, Dortmund educational scientist Franco Rest answered the question of whether children need a period of several hours every day in a room with a class/group of other similar-aged children in order to socialize healthily with a 'rather not.' "Such a time period with 20 to 25 similar aged individuals could even have considerable and serious damages as a consequence," writes Rest in the study, above all in the case of especially sensitive children. [84] For that reason, he is for the legalization of State-controlled nonschool learning.[85]

A 2008 dissertation written at Marburg University by social scientist Thomas Spiegler, who teaches in Friedensau, was honored by the Society for Sociology in 2010. [86] Using the methods of social science, he for the first time empirically investigated what becomes of German homeschoolers and has been unable to determine any sort of threatening scenarios or disadvantages.

---

[82]   Volker Ladenthin, *Homeschooling—Fragen und Antworten: Häusliche Bildung im Spannungsfeld zwischen Schulpflicht und Elternrecht. Pädagogik in Europa in Geschichte und Gegenwart 2* (Bonn: VKW, 2010).

[83]   Hanniel Strebel, *Home Education—Verteidigung eines alternativen Bildungskonzepts und Lebensstils unter besonderer Berücksichtigung der Schweiz* (VKW: Bonn, 2011).

[84]   Birgitta vom Lehn, "Das fliehende Klassenzimmer," *Welt am Sonntag* April 5, 2009: http://www.welt.de/wams_print/article3505082/Das-fliehende-Klassenzimmer. html. See also Dr. Franco Rest, "Brauchen Kinder den täglichen mehrstündigen Aufenthalt in einem Raum mit einer Klasse / Gruppe anderer Gleichaltriger, um sich gesund zu sozialisieren?" Gutachten 2009: http://www.netzwerk-bildungsfreiheit.de/pdf/Gutachten%20Prof_Rest%20Sozialisation.pdf.

[85]   Rest, "'Bildungspflicht' als 'Schulzwang' und die Liquidation des Elternrechts in Deutschland," Lecture (2008). See also "Homeschooling—Häuslicher Unterricht: Ein Schritt zur Anpassung des Deutschen Erziehungs- und Bildungswesens an die Menschenrechte," Lecture (2008), http://www.homeschooling.de/sites/default/files/ documents/vortrag_rest.pdf.

[86]   Thomas Spiegler, *Home Education in Deutschland: Hintergründe – Praxis – Entwicklung*, (Wiesbaden: VS Verlag für Sozialwiss, 2008).

Spiegler, who has been interviewed by large daily newspapers,[87] holds lectures on the topic at numerous universities and at scholarly symposia in Germany,[88] and has put out an impressive list of essays in professional journals since 2005 up to the present time.[89] Spiegler's results match the results of similar studies in other countries.[90]

While I have been writing these lines, one of the largest German daily newspapers, and perhaps the most intellectually oriented one, has published a positive article about homeschooling.[91] The newspaper simply interviewed a 22-year-old controller for an industrial company who completed her German general qualification studies for university entrance (German: *Abitur*) with a grade point average of 1.8 (based on a German scale where 1.0 is the highest possible grade and 6.0 the lowest) and went on to study business administration. She not only reports on her own positive experiences but also on those of her siblings.

How can it otherwise be explained that the Germany Railways' (Die Deutsche Bahn) *Mobil* magazine printed a longer excerpt from the work of Canadian author David Gilmour? Gilmour has written a book about the idea of taking his school-tired son out of school and rhapsodizes about the school-free time (*Unser allerbestes Jahr*, Fischer Publishing, 2009; title translation: *Our Best Year of All*). The French author André Stern, 38, belabors a school-free zone in a book (. . . *und ich war nie in der Schule*, Za-

---

[87] E.g., "Erfolgreich lernen ohne Schule," Interview with Thomas Spiegler, *Welt am Sonntag* February 3, 2008: http://www.welt.de/wams_print/article1626933/Erfolg reich_lernen_ohne_Schule.html.

[88] See http://www.thh-friedensau.de/dozentenseiten/spiegler/035_Vortraege/index.html.

[89] See http://www.thh-friedensau.de/dozentenseiten/spiegler/030_Publikationen/index. html.

[90] Most of these are discussed in my book. Of late, there are two Canadian studies worthy of recommendation: Deani A. Neven Van Pelt et al, *Fifteen Years Later: Home-Educated Canadian Adults* (Vancouver: Canadian Centre for Home Education, 2009): http://www.hslda.ca/cche_research/2009Study.pdf ; and Patrick Basham et al, *Home Schooling: From the Extreme to the Mainstream* October 2007: http://www.fraserinstitute.org/research-news/display.aspx?id=13089. See also Alan Thomas, *Bildung zu Hause* (Leipzig: Tologo, 2007, also at Google Books), an investigation of 100 families in England and Australia—incidentally with a preface by Prof. Dr. Wolfgang Hinte, acting director of the Institut für Stadtteilbezogene Soziale Arbeit und Beratung (ISSAB, an institute addressing neighborhood-based social work and counseling) at the University of Duisburg-Essen.

[91] Katrin Hummel, "Wir mussten uns verstecken: Eine Homeschoolerin erzählt," *Frankfurt Allgemeine Zeitung* June 20, 2011: http://www.faz.net/artikel/C31206/ eine-homeschoolerin-erzaehlt-wir-mussten-uns-verstecken-30387786.html; see also Thomas, "Bildung zu Hause."

bert Sandmann, 2009). Patrick Meinhardt, the education spokesman for the FDP parliamentary faction, sees it similarly. "I would like not to prevent homeschooling and can imagine that instruction at home is doable if it is subject to state control and if the qualification of the people to whom the child relates most closely is ensured . . ." In any event, Meinhardt pleads for drawing homeschooling out of illegality: "I see great opportunities to do much within a controlled context."[92]

It is at this point that research and politics have to start: What becomes of homeschoolers, and how do these individuals view homeschooling later as adults? Instead of empirical facts, many would rather begin with scare tactics that depict what allegedly has to happen—without any proof and as if negative appearances are not found in the public education system. Or they play on fears of what would happen if fundamentalist Muslims were to conduct homeschooling—as if this trend actually existed. Additionally, they speak as if we otherwise prohibit everything which such fundamentalists could derive benefit from and as if it would be better if these same people would instead open private schools.

A good example for the tactics to create panic instead of using the results of empirical investigations is the president of the German Teachers' Association, who conceals that in the process he is carrying on partisan lobbying efforts. "In any case, Josef Kraus holds Rest's argumentation for 'not comprehensible.'" The president of the German Teachers' Association in fact fears a 'cementing of class-specific socialization': "Imagine that fundamentalist Islamic parents were to conduct homeschooling. There would then be many children, above all girls, who would no longer learn a word of German."

The parliamentary CDU faction also sees it this way. Their spokesman for education policy, Stefan Müller, has said, "If we were even just to allow homeschooling to a limited extent, our integration efforts would be counteracted."[93]

In addition to the above works authored by professors, there are continually other academic theses being produced with results that are favorable for homeschooling.[94] Besides that, there are naturally legal opinions from ongoing proceedings that are to be mentioned.[95]

---

[92] Birgitta vom Lehn, "Das fliehende Klassenzimmer," *Welt Online* April 4, 2009: http://www.welt.de/wams_print/article3505082/Das-fliehende-Klassenzimmer.html.

[93] Ibid.

[94] E.g., B. Stefan Schönenberger, "Homeschooling auf dem Prüfstand," Masterarbeit an der Pädagogischen Hochschule Zentralschweiz (Luzern, 2010): http://edudoc.ch/record/82085/files/MA-Homeschooling.pdf   and   Alexander

Paragraph 1666 is Misused

Completely in contrast to all of the above are intensified efforts from the side of the authorities and courts over the last 10 years against homeschooling. Regardless of how one assesses it, homeschooling and missing students are exclusively assessed against the legal situation, not against any educational or other measures. Against this assessment, the homeschoolers, who study hard after all, are worse off than truants.

Thomas Spiegler correctly asks whether education can be a legal offense.[96] If it only were to stay at the level of a misdemeanor! In the meantime it is Paragraph 1666a of the Civil Law Code which has evolved into the standard procedure against homeschoolers, though never created for this purpose.

The usual application of Paragraph 1666a (1) and (2) in the Civil Law Code, which addresses cases where parents do not send their children to school (or force them to attend school), and which should be used in order to take custody of the children away from the parents, is in my view completely inappropriate in the case of providing school instruction at home.[97] It actually refers to parents who neglect the well-being of their children and for whom (1) other measures do not come into question or (2) where other measures remain unsuccessful. The child's well-being falls completely out of view. This is due to the fact that the situation practically exclusively has to do with intact families, and except for homeschooling, as a general rule, no other form of neglect can and is charged against the parents. Should it, however, serve the well-being of the child and the pedagogical mandate of the State for the child to be picked up by the police and thenceforth for months—or even for years—to be placed in a home without contact with parents? That children in good health have to be repeatedly subjected to psychological and psychiatric reviewers and—mostly with wrong motives—interrogated about their parents? That the children, against their declared will, are forced into what is for them an unknown school—again of-

    Klaehr, "Über die Zusammenhänge von Herrschaft und Bildung," Bachelor-Arbeit (Potsdam: Universität Potsdam, 2008): http://opus.kobv.de/ubp/volltexte/2008/2445/pdf/klaehr_bachelor.pdf.

[95]   Johannes Goldbecher, "Homeschooling in Deutschland," Rechtsgutachten (2007): http://www.homeschooling.de/sites/default/files/documents/vortrag_rest.pdf.

[96]   Thomas Spiegler, "Kann Ordnungswidrigkeit Bildung sein? Das Spannungsfeld zwischen Home Education und Schulpflicht in Deutschland aus soziologischer Perspektive," *Recht der Jugend und des Bildungswesens* 53, no. 1 (2005): 71–82.

[97]   See Renata Leuffen, *Natürlich ohne Schule leben* (Bonn: Kid-Verlag, 1993), 6.

ten under police force—and have to experience their parents going to jail? All for the well-being of the child? No. Rather for the well-being of the system!

One does not have to be in favor of homeschooling in order to recognize a misuse of § 1666a and to reject such a criminalization of keenly culturally minded parents. In my view, the removal of custody rights, prison, fines, and police coercion associated with forcing children who are well-instructed to go to school is not in proportion to the spirit of the law, but rather a brutish and brawny display of State power.

Just so that no one misunderstands: not everything parents do for a better future for their children is to be endorsed. However, I am of the opinion that one should deal with this natural parental instinct with more reverence. Parents who want something different are not to be placed on the same level as parents who are violent and let their children get into a bad state and who are rightly punished.

Given the threat of the removal of custody and the experience that children are actually suddenly placed in homes and forced from there to go to school, many parents have moved to the neighboring countries of Austria or the Netherlands. Children achieve their school degrees there without any problems and then have an apprenticeship or go on to study. As an alternative, they emigrate to Canada or to the USA—recently there was a celebrated case where a German family for this reason was granted asylum in the USA.[98] The case in Germany is that homeschooled children want homeschooling and are not forced to do it, which would not practically be possible anyway, and when placed in homes, they do not see their parents for months or for years. It is, by the way, not the worst and the dumbest who leave Germany, as it is when the loss of religious minorities or very independent portions of a population hurt more than help a country.

When looking across Europe and worldwide—apart from some dictatorships—Germany is an anomaly with its absolute prohibition of any form of home instruction, enforced by penalty.[99] Just to add some supplemen-

---

[98]   "Homeschooling Family Granted Political Asylum," *Home School Legal Defense Association* January 26, 2010: http://www.hslda.org/hs/international/Germany/201 001260.asp. See also Tristana Moore, "Give me your tired, your poor, your homeschoolers," *TIME* March 8, 2010: http://www.time.com/time/magazine/article /0,9171,1968099,00.html.

[99]   This is documented in detail by Amanda J. Petrie, "Home Educators and the Law within Europe," *International Review of Education—Internationale Zeitschrift für Erziehungswissenschaft* 41, no. 3/4 (1995): 285–296. See also "Home Education in Europe and the Implementation of Changes to the Law," *International Review of Education* 47, no. 5 (2001): 477–500. [Both essays are found in a German

tary information, Germany's dominating behavior over private schools has had the consequence that Germany has the lowest percentage of private schools of all free countries on earth.[100]

The international OECD (Organisation for Economic Co-operation and Development) considers home instruction to be part of the normal educational offerings in Europe and worldwide, as found in the OECD's German language version of free school choice and private school pleadings published by the German Federal Ministry of Education.[101] It is astonishing that this is forbidden in Germany in contrast to the rest of Europe. This report shows above all how isolated Germany is with its uniform school system, while worldwide the education of children and adolescents is being increasingly decentralized, privatized, and pluralized.

Responding Educationally

One often reacts to publicly known truants in a very engaged and sacrificial manner, with special educational programs and not with threats and reprisals.[102]

---

translation under: Thomas Schirrmacher (ed.), *Wenn Kinder zu Hause zur Schule gehen: Dokumentation* (Nürnberg: VTR, 2004.)] The British secular educational researcher Amanda J. Petrie is the leading authority for Europe in this area; compare Petrie, "Home Education and the Local Education Authority" (University of Liverpool, 1992) and "Home Education and the Law," *Education and the Law* 10 (1998): 123–135. See also "The Prevalence of Home Education in England," Report to the Department for Education and Employment (London, 1999). Compare also Cynthia Guttmann, "European Disunity," *Unesco Courier* (June 2000), 15: http://unesdoc.unesco.org/images/0011/001199/119966e.pdf.

[100] OECD, "Freie Schulwahl im internationalen Vergleich," *Bildungsforschung internationaler Organisationen* 14 (Frankfurt: Peter Lang, 1996), 96–102 (published by the German Institute for International Education [Deutsches Institut für internationale Bildung] on behalf of the Federal Ministry of Education [Bundesministeriums für Bildung].

[101] _____, *School: A Matter of Choice* (Paris: OECD, 1994). See also OECD, "Freie Schulwahl ...Vergleich."

[102] Compare dissertation by Kirsten Puhr, *Lernangebote für schulverweigernde Kinder und Jugendliche: Pädagogische Probleme unter dem Anspruch von Schulpflicht und Bildungsrecht* (Hamburg: Kovach, 2003), 107. See also Christoph Ehmann and Hermann Rademacker (eds.), *Schulversäumnisse und sozialer Ausschluss* (Bielefeld: Deutsches Institut für Erwachsenenbildung, 2003), 59–106. A shorter, excellent overview of such measures is found in Maria Schreiber-Kittl, "Konzepte und Maßnahmen gegen Schulverweigerung," *Recht der Jugend und des Bildungswesens* 49, no. 2 (2001): 225–238.

Why can there not be just as much flexibility and creativity with homeschoolers? Attempts are made to make education palatable to the pupils affected by using programs, since one knows that permanent reprisals do not work[103] and that one can hardly have children taken to school by the police every day and, in the best case, guarded there. However, why act contrary to the actual legal situation and offer truants expensive (and sensible!) social-pedagogical programs, while in the case of supporters of home educational instruction no exceptions come to mind?

One should go and read what a basic advocate of State-coerced school attendance, Wilhelm Habermalz, wrote in the magazine entitled *Recht der Jugend und des Bildungswesens (The Right of Youth and of the Educational System)*, which up until now had always been against schooling at home. [104] He writes: "It is in fact nowadays hardly justifiable to speak of an educational reason for the State using police force to get delinquent pupils to go to school."[105] This has little purpose, since from experience this has to be repeated daily. He summarizes: "The rules for implementing compulsory education are on the whole highly 'in need of overhaul.' There are in part legal misgivings that can be raised—for instance the threat of punishment against the school-aged—and the use thereof is to some extent dispensed with. This is due to the fact that its result is ineffective—such as, for example, compelling students to go to school."[106]

German compulsory school attendance means an unnecessary criminalization of parents and children. The State should solve educational problems educationally, not with court judgments, prison sentences, and deploying police.[107] There are enough educational studies which hold compulsory school attendance to be the wrong way to go.[108] In conversation or in podium discussions on the radio or television, I have repeatedly observed that professors of education and other experts who speak out

---

[103] Compare for instance Lutz R. Reuter and Xinke Zhang, "Zur Schulpflicht von Minderheiten- und Zuwandererkindern im deutschen Schulwesen," *Beiträge aus dem Bereich Pädagogik* (Hamburg: Universität der Bundeswehr, 1997), 33.

[104] Wilhelm Habermalz, "Geldbuße und Schulzwang—die andere Seite der Schulpflicht: Über das Instrumentarium des Staates zur Durchsetzung der Schulpflicht," *Recht der Jugend und des Bildungswesens* 49, no. 2 (2001): 218–224.

[105] Ibid, 218.

[106] Ibid, 224.

[107] The possible measures are listed in: Habermalz, "Geldbuße und Schulzwang."

[108] Siegfried Lamnek, *Wider den Schulzwang: Ein sekundäranalytischer Beitrag zur Delinquenz und Kriminalisierung Jugendlicher* (München, 1985). See alsoWolfgang Sachs, *Schulzwang und soziale Kontrolle: Argumente für eine Entschulung des Lernens* (Dissertation, Frankfurt: University of Tübingen, 1976).

against homeschooling are still of the opinion that penalties, the police, and prison are not the solution for dealing with homeschoolers and only injure the children involved.

Representatives of State compulsory school attendance mostly argue with an alleged superior form of education. I cannot understand what having screaming children wrested from their parents and forcibly taken in a police car to a school from which they would run at the first opportunity should have to do with education and the well-being of a child. It in fact does not have to do with education or the well-being of children but is rather about power, control, and worldview.

The Many True Truants

The State should deal with the many true truants who do not have an educational future instead of targeting the very few homeschooled children. And it should ask itself what it is doing wrong that leads so many to skip school, since in the meantime it is not only the lazy and criminal who are missing, but also many who are mobbed, who fear violence, who have a school phobia diagnosed by doctors, who are not keeping up in school, or who as highly gifted or as those plagued with learning difficulties do not receive sufficient personal encouragement.[109]

Raimund Pousset, who wants to do away with compulsory education in order to retain the State school system, points to the failure of the State school system that above all goes back to the absolutism of supra-regional authorities and State coercion in the local school. About 4 million functional analphabets, 90,000 school-leavers annually with no degree, street children and foreigners who have never been registered, 250,000 repeaters annually,[110] and, above, all the gigantic market for private tutoring with over € 1 billion in revenues, and a de facto introduction of school fees[111] show that compulsory education under penalty of law does not deliver what it promises and that our neighboring countries do better without this coercion.

According to an estimate by Spiegel, there are in Germany about 250,000 school-age children who practically continually skip school.[112]

---

[109] Compare the excellent compilation in: Maria Schreiber-Kittl, "Alles Versager? Schulverweigerung im Urteil von Experten," Arbeitspapier (München/Leipzig: Deutsches Jugendinstitut, 2001).

[110] Raimund Pousset, *Schafft die Schulpflicht ab!* (Frankfurt: Eichborn, 2000), 32–35.

[111] Ibid, 32.

[112] *Der Spiegel* 20 (2002), 140–141.

The most thorough investigation made of the topic dates to 2003. It documents how the Ministry of Education does not collect a number of truants that can be taken seriously and that most schools likewise to do not have reliable numbers![113] Authors have come to the following conclusion: "What has been missing up to now is the general recognition of a need for political action on educational policy."[114] We in Germany are reaching peaks in Europe, whereby in Europe the percentage of truants is lower the more local administration and school self-determination prevail and the weaker central State school oversight is.[115]

All of these children do not receive education at home. The courts and the police would have a lot to do if these children were all forced into schools, and it is certain that the crime rate would actually sink if all these children were in school. According to the legal requirements, the authorities should be sending parents notices for fines of tens of thousands of Euros.

According to statements made by the Federal Ministry of Education and the German Federal Statistical Office, out of all school-leavers in 1998 who were at the end of their period of compulsory education, 9% or 83,000 did not receive a school degree, and of those two-thirds were boys.[116] Up to 1997 the rate was at 8.8% (approximately 79,000) and by 2000 rose to 9.2% (86,600).[117] "About one-third of school-leavers from general education schools without a secondary education degree achieve this at a later time at a vocational school."[118] This means that about 60,000 adolescents annually who will never achieve a school degree in their life.

However, those who get into trouble with the authorities, the justice system, and the police are not the 250,000 truants and their parents or legal guardians, and are not those responsible for the fact that annually there are 60,000 children who will never receive a school degree. Rather, it is people

---

[113] See the excerpts from a document by the Education Minister in: Ehmann and Rademacker, *Schulversäumnisse und sozialer Ausschluss*, 71–72. The authors are advocates of compulsory school attendance. They present the investigations of recent years, which sought to capture the rate of truants.

[114] Ibid, 16.

[115] Ibid, 107–119.

[116] German Federal Ministry of Education (BMBF), *Grund- und Strukturdaten*, BMBF Publik 1999/2000, 80. See also German Federal Statistics Office (ed.), *Datenreport 2002*/Schriftenreihe 376 (Bonn: Bundeszentrale für politische Bildung, 2002), 62.

[117] Ibid, 61–62.

[118] Ibid, 62. A listing according to German federal states, cities, and administrative districts for the year 2001 can be found at www.apoll-online.de/bildungsdaten.html.

who do not neglect their children, despite the fact that one does not have to worry about the education of these children—at least this is the global experience with homeschoolers.

Freedom of Religion Also Belongs within the Realm of Education

"No person shall be denied the right to education. In the exercise of any functions which it assumes in relation to education and to teaching, the State shall respect the right of parents to ensure such education and teaching in conformity with their own religions and philosophical convictions" (Article 2 of the European Convention on Human Rights).

Only in Germany is the area of education almost completely removed from the area of religious freedom.[119] The right parents have to not only raise their children but also to determine and shape their religion, in fact does not count in the area of schooling in Germany. Indeed, even if it is the children themselves who for religious reasons refuse certain things, their conscience is not protected in the school. In all of Europe and in all democratic countries on earth, the sphere of school is a space in which the religion and conscience of parents and children should be and are taken into account.

In the generally simple Protocol entitled "Enforcement of certain rights and freedoms" as attached to the European Convention on Human Rights, which is legally binding for Germany, of the Council of Europe dated March 20, 1952, one reads in Article 2, "No person shall be denied the right to education. In the exercise of any functions which it assumes in relation to education and to teaching, the State shall respect the right of parents to ensure such education and teaching in conformity with their own religions and philosophical convictions." In Germany, this European human right is de facto treated as if it were nothing.

Make Exceptions!

One could, without a change to the law for exceptions, already allow homeschooling. In each case, around the wording that sets general compulsory school attendance, all state constitutions and compulsory education laws state that only the educational authorities may allow exceptions. Rep-

---

[119] Compare to the situation in the USA: Rosemary Salomone, "Home Schooling and Religious Freedom," *Education Week* no. 8, October 20, 2004: 52, 41.

resentatively, one can quote § 76, Paragraph 1, Sentence 1 of the education act of Baden-Wuerttemberg, which says that is it mandatory for children to attend school, "as long as their upbringing and instruction in another form has not sufficiently been provided for." For grammar school, § 76, Paragraph 1, Sentence 2 applies more closely: "In the place of attendance at a grammar school, other types of instruction may only be allowed in special cases by the educational authorities." Without this exemption clause, things just do not work. Otherwise, one would have to force seriously ill and mentally handicapped children to attend school, and do likewise with German children living overseas, pregnant teenagers, or children with a school phobia.

In most locations in Germany—and mostly purposely not made publicly known—educational instruction at home is tolerated or permitted. I have in any event a number of acquaintances for whom this is the case, among them welfare recipients as well as professors. In short: Even if it is theoretically settled that the school authorities have the right to force all children into school, they *do not have to* do that. They can make exceptions. In several hundred cases in Germany, it is, in my opinion, more reasonable to allow exceptions and to check whether the children actually are learning at home than to conduct an educational battle geared toward media attention.

By the way, Lower Saxony is very generous with such exceptions and for that reason has never had a homeschooling case that was controversial and made good press copy. Lower Saxony's § 63, Paragraph 5 of the Education Act states: "Private instruction may only be allowed to school-aged children throughout the first six grades in the place of school attendance in exceptional cases." In addition there is the following waiver: "Fulfillment of compulsory education by private instruction (§ 63, Paragraph 5). The fulfillment of the obligation to attend school is only permitted in exceptional cases in the first six school grades and is only to be granted if the instruction fulfills requirements that are placed upon the corresponding type of school . . ."[120]

Homeschooling as an Alternative for Special Cases

Homeschooling is an alternative for many children who could only fulfill the compulsory school attendance requirement with difficulty. The State has to make an astonishing number of exceptions to compulsory schooling,

---

[120] Quoted from the Ministry's website on law relating to school: www.schure.de/2241001/0035074.htm (accessed April 1, 2005).

whereby at this point the federal states all proceed very differently. Many homeschooling cases begin unwillingly with such difficult situations. "Many pupils are instructed in their parents' home for practical reasons— also as an interim solution," declares Thomas Spiegler of the University of Marburg, who is working on a doctoral dissertation on the topic of home education in Germany . . . Children with fear of school, psychosomatic disorders, and those who have experienced mobbing can learn stress-free at home. However, it also does less talented and highly gifted children good to have a free choice regarding their pace of learning. A child who at the age of three is playing chess and gives his first piano concert at the age of six can almost be mentally destroyed with regular lessons, according to the reported experience of a mother . . ."[121]

It is a known fact that there have always been exceptions for the long-term ill.[122] Why, however, stop school teachers from giving regular instruction and not involve the parents, etc. where they desire this? Would not instruction at home be a better alternative for a number of ADHD children, the handicapped, children with learning difficulties, etc. than a special school? What is to be done with children overseas, with children whose parents are continually traveling in connection with their careers, the children of showmen and circus artists? What is to be done with highly gifted children or children with a school phobia? The State either exercises coercion or has to provide costly alternatives. In our neighboring countries, homeschooling is always an alternative in such cases. Homeschooling is always an alternative if parents want to give their children an individual choice that a large system has difficulty offering.

For example, it has been demonstrated that schooling at home presents a very good solution for ADHD children and children with similar prob-

---

[121] Lioba Schafnitzel, "Nie wieder in die Schule! Hausunterricht: Erfolgreich, aber in Deutschland verboten," *Nürnberger Zeitung* April 29, 2004: www.hausunterricht.org/html/nz-konferenz.html.

[122] Compare as available examples printed coincidentally—all ministries of education provide information: The Minister of Education of North Rhine Westphalia [Kultusminister des Landes Nordrhein-Westfalen] (ed.), *Richtlinien für die Schule für Kranke (Sonderschule) und für den Hausunterricht in Nordrhein-Westfalen* (October 24, 1984); *Die Schule in Nordrhein-Westfalen* 6601 (Köln: Greven, 1985), 8; *Handreichung Krankenhaus- und Hausunterricht* (Kultusministerium Rheinland-Pfalz: Mainz, 1990), 54; *Bildungswege in Nordrhein-Westfalen— Sonderschulen: Schule für Blinde, für Sehbehinderte, für Gehörlose, für Schwerhörige, für Körperbehinderte, für Sprachbehinderte, für Erziehungshilfe, für Lernbehinderte, für Geistigbehinderte, Krankenhausschule und Hausunterricht* (Düsseldorf: Der Kultusminister des Landes Nordrhein-Westfalen, 1981) 45.

lems.[123] Here in Germany, the enormous effort on the part of parents is appreciated very little. Rather, the problem is heaped upon overburdened teachers who have 30 other children in their class, or the child is sent to a special school where he does not belong.

Compulsory School Attendance Is a Child of Absolutism

What in legal German used to be designated compulsory education (*Schulzwang*) and is now referred to as compulsory school attendance is not a child of democracy but rather the child of princely absolutism.

Indeed, this is self-evident for historians, but it is often willingly presented in another way. Let us listen to an advocate of compulsory education as a proxy for practically every presentation of the history of school in Germany: "The installation of a publicly supervised basic school education of youth and the assurance of it through compulsory school and instruction, compulsory school attendance, and punishment find their origins in the welfare state and police maxims of enlightened absolutism. The justification of the State to ultimately threaten and then exercise State power so that the individual is forced to go to school has been justified since that time in different ways, but principally it has rarely been questioned."[124]

Princes wanted all subjects to be good citizens and youth to be raised to be good soldiers. "For the first time, as far as I can see, the principle of compulsory education is expressed in the Weimar School Regulations of 1619."[125] Even though educational instruction at home was nevertheless able to have a niche existence, it is still the case that compulsory education as it developed did not serve the august democratic goals of equality and equal opportunity. Rather, it was a central and controlling element with which the State educated the population in accordance with its principles. "Compulsory school attendance is the child of absolutism."[126] For that rea-

---

[123] Leonore Colacion Hayes, *Homeschooling the Child with ADD (or other special needs): Your Complete Guide to Successfully Homeschooling the Child with Learning Differences* (Roseville, CA: Prima Publ., 2002).

[124] Winter, "Schulpflicht und Schulzwang," 408–423. Similarly Leongard Froese, "Bildungspolitische Entwicklungsskizze," quoted in Leonhard Froese and Werner Krawietz (ed.), *Deutsche Schulgesetzgebung. Band I: Brandenburg, Preußen und Deutsches Reich bis 1945* (Weinheim: Beltz, 1968), 11–45.

[125] Friedrich Paulsen, *Das deutsche Bildungswesen in seiner geschichtlichen Entwicklung* (Darmstadt: Wissenschaftliche Buchgesellschaft, 1966), 85.

[126] Hans Moller, "Die Schulpflicht als Rechtsaltertum," quoted in Johannes Heimrath (ed.), *Die Entfesselung der Kreativität: Das Menschenrecht auf Schulvermeidung* (Wolfratshausen: Drachen Verlag, 1991), 39.

son, a direct pathway leads from compulsory education to National Socialism.[127] National Socialism made use of the fact that in any case all children had to learn according to the manner the State prescribed, and thus it merely eliminated or harmonized remaining free alternatives in private and alternative schools as well as in home educational instruction. "Instead of that, general compulsory education, while rolling back private schools and private instruction, opened the way to National Socialism's giving an ideological attitude to school."[128]

Raimund Pousset, who is a passionate teacher in the service of the State, calls the State-run school in Germany a "sluggish school system from the pre-democratic imperial age"[129] on the basis of its overall inflexible structure, rigid leadership through greatly remote educational authorities, and the belief that the State alone can guarantee children a future.

In the name of tolerance and integration, homeschoolers are intolerantly forced into school. We pride ourselves in Germany for our tolerance, but in reality we have more laws enforceable by penalties and fewer freedoms in many areas than at the time of the emperors.

Compulsory Education in Germany Is Also a Legacy of National Socialism

In Germany, and in spite of all compulsory school attendance laws, educational instruction in the home was always permitted as an exception prior to 1938.[130]

Germany, which always had the strictest such laws since the introduction of compulsory school attendance in Prussia in 1717,[131] nevertheless did not have a prohibition on private or home educational instruction up to the time of the Weimar Constitution in 1919 and the conclusive Prussian[132] compulsory school attendance law dating to 1927. Private and home forms

---

[127] See also Froese, "Bildungspolitische Entwicklungsskizze."

[128] Moller, "Die Schulpflicht als Rechtsaltertum," 40.

[129] Pousset, *Schafft die Schulpflicht ab!*, 41.

[130] See also Horst Schiffler and Rolf Winkeler, *Tausend Jahre Schule: Eine Kulturgeschichte des Lernens in Bildern* (Stuttgart: Belser, 1985), 90.

[131] Compare to compulsory education in German law from the Middle Ages until today by Albrecht Mors, "Die Entwicklung der Schulpflicht in Deutschland," (Dissertation, Dr. iur.: Tübingen, 1986). See also Ekkehart Stein and Monika Roell, *Handbuch des Schulrechts* (Köln: Heymanns, 1988) 52–53 and often; Hermann Avenarius, *Schulrechtskunde* (Neuwied: Luchterhand, 2000), 311–325.

[132] Compare Stein and Roell, *Handbuch des Schulrechts*, 52–53.

of educational instruction were still widespread. In the so-called Constitution of St. Paul's Church (*Paulskirchenverfassung*), the imperial constitution of March 28, 1849, home educational instruction was still found in the human rights catalog in § 154: "Instruction in the home is subject to no limitation."[133] In all the strict Prussian regulations, home educational instruction continued to nonetheless be allowed, e.g., in Prussia's *General-Land-Schul-Reglement* (General State School Regulations) dated August 12, 1763 (§ 15)[134] or in the *Schulordnung für die Elementarschulen der Provinz Preußen* (School Regulations for Elementary Schools in the Province of Prussia) dated December 11, 1845 (§ 1)[135] in the *Kabinettsorder betr. die Schulzucht* (Cabinet Order relating to Child Rearing in School) dated May 14, 1825: "Parents, or their legal representatives who are unable to demonstrate that they are providing for the necessary instruction of children in their house should be admonished via means of compulsion and penalties to send every child who has completed his fifth year of life to school.[136]

The *Handbook of School Law* correctly summarized: "Strictly speaking, into the 20th century compulsory education was not compulsion to attend a public school but rather only meant compulsory instruction."[137]

Radical German compulsory education was first introduced in this form in 1938 by the National Socialists solely in order to control German youth. For the first time in the law relating to compulsory education in the German Reich (the *Reichsschulpflichtgesetz* or Compulsory Education Law of the Reich) dated July 6, 1938 (amended on May 16, 1941),[138] it was set down that pupils were allowed by police action to be forced into instruction and that legal guardians could be punished with monetary fines and imprisonment if they did not enforce this with their children. Section 1 reads as follows: "(1) General compulsory education. General compulsory education exists in the German Reich. It ensures education and training in the spirit of National Socialism. All children and adolescents with German

---

[133] *Deutsche Verfassungen* (München: Wilhelm Goldmann, 1974), 32. State supervision of schools is found in § 153.

[134] Froese and Krawietz, *Deutsche Schulgesetzgebung*, 107.

[135] Ibid, 155.

[136] Ibid, 152.

[137] Stein and Roell, *Handbuch des Schulrechts*, 52. Compare Petrie, "Home Educators and the Law within Europe," 285-287.

[138] Froese and Krawietz, *Deutsche Schulgesetzgebung*, 224–226. See also www.verfassungen.de/de/de33-45/schulpflicht38.htm, which makes the differences between the July 6, 1938 and May 16, 1941 versions very clear (accessed May 1, 2005).

nationality who have their home or habitual residence domestically are subject to it." Even here there is immediate mention of exceptions, since in § 12 it reads as follows: "Compulsory education is fulfilled by attending a school of the German Reich. Any exceptions are decided upon by the educational authorities." And § 5 reads: "Fulfillment of the people's compulsory education. (1) All children are obligated to attend elementary school insofar as their upbringing and education is not sufficiently provided for in another manner. (2) During the first four years of elementary school, another form of instruction in the place of attendance at an elementary school is only permitted in special cases on an exceptional basis" (all the aforementioned items are from the 1938 version).

Decisive for the implementation of "education . . . in the spirit of National Socialism," however, was § 12: "Compulsory school attendance. Children and adolescents who do not fulfill the obligation to attend an elementary or vocational training school will be forced to attend the school. In this connection the aid of the police can be made use of." Through the law dated May 16, 1941, § 12 Sentence 1 received the following mitigated version: "Children and adolescents who do not fulfill the obligation to attend an elementary school, secondary school, or vocational training school will be brought to the school by force."

In short: "Not until the Reich Compulsory Education Law dated July 6, 1938, which for the first time governed compulsory school attendance, were consequences intended for truants . . . "[139] The central importance of this law is also expressed in the fact that compulsory mandatory vocational school was for the first time regulated and for the first time employers and apprentices' employers could be punished if their apprentices, etc., did not go to vocational school.[140]

The National Socialist's Reich Compulsory Education Law was unfortunately adopted by the federal states and not rolled back. It applied in the federal states in unchanged form for a long time.

In 1975, the failure to fulfill the requirement of compulsory school attendance was downgraded from a criminal offense to a legal infraction, but in tough cases in the city-states, Hessen, Saarland, and Mecklenburg-West Pomerania, the status of a simple legal infraction can be exceeded. From 1938 to 1974, the failure to fulfill the compulsory education requirement was a criminal offense—in Saarland, that is still the case today. Within the framework of sweeping penal reform, in almost all federal states the failure to meet the requirement of compulsory education since the Second Penal

---

[139] Habermalz, "Geldbuße und Schulzwang," 218.
[140] See also Mors, "Die Entwicklung der Schulpflicht in Deutschland," 261.

Law Reform Act on January 1, 1975, became only a legal infraction.[141] At that time, what had existed until then as a "violation," where the extent of the punishment was between a legal infraction and a criminal offense, was abolished, and all federal states had to decide whether they wanted to upgrade or downgrade that "violation."

It is in fact the case that homeschoolers are still not treated as if a legal infraction is being dealt with. Rather, it is as if they are criminal offenders where the extent of the punishment is escalated and in the end is de facto still too severe. I do not mean this in the formal juridical sense, but whoever is subjected to a barrage of monetary penalty charge notices, public threats by politicians in the media, proceedings to take away children's custody, having police in one's house, and being imprisoned, truly no longer has the impression of having only committed a legal infraction. In my opinion, people are de facto made into criminals, although penal law reform should have led to a decriminalization.

---

[141] Habermalz, "Geldbuße und Schulzwang," 218.

The Justification of Homeschooling Vis-A-Vis the European Human Rights System

by John Warwick Montgomery

Introduction

The European Court of Human Rights has taken no official position on the legitimacy of homeschooling, so it may appear premature to raise the question in that context. However, a related case, brought by parents to the Strasbourg Court in 2003 against the German government was declared inadmissible in 2006, and the unpublished opinion suggests that Strasbourg does not view the choice of homeschooling as a parental or a children's right. The opinion reads in part:

The Court observes . . . that there appears to be no consensus among the Contracting States with regard to compulsory attendance of primary schools. While some countries permit home education, other States provide for compulsory attendance of its State or private schools.

In the present case, the Court notes that the German authorities and courts have carefully reasoned their decisions and mainly stressed the fact that not only the acquisition of knowledge, but also the integration into and first experience with society are important goals in primary school education. The German courts found that those objectives cannot be equally met by home education even if it allowed children to acquire the same standard of knowledge as provided for by primary school education. The Court considers this presumption as not being erroneous and as falling within the Contracting States' margin of appreciation which they enjoy in setting up and interpreting rules for their education systems. The Federal Constitutional Court stressed the general interest of society to avoid the emergence of parallel societies based on separate philosophical convictions and the importance of integrating minorities into society.[142]

---

[142] *Konrad and Others v.Germany,* Application No. 35504/03 (11 September 2006), 7–8. It must be emphasised that this is an unpublished opinion, not appearing in the HUDOC database, and therefore does not constitute any kind of legal precedent, internationally or nationally. No homeschooling case appears in the authoritative list of cases dealing with "Le Droit à l'Instruction (Article 2 du Protocole no. 1)" in Vincent Berger, *Jurisprudence de la Cour Européenne des Droits de l'Homme* (11th ed.; Paris: Sirey/Dalloz, 2009), 625–43.

Even though these remarks create no precedent for subsequent cases before the Strasbourg Court, and even though the waters were clearly muddied in this application by applicants' arguments based on their opposition to "sex education [and] the appearance of mythical creatures such as witches and dwarfs in fairytales during school lessons,"[143] it is clear that the issue of homeschooling will not go away in the European context—especially owing to the almost fanatical opposition to it on the part of governmental authorities in Germany and Sweden. We therefore see the matter as worthy of treatment here.

Let us begin with larger—more abstract and philosophical—aspects of the problem before analyzing the issue in the European human rights context.

Philosophical Considerations and Their Relevance to Homeschooling

There are three major positions possible in justifying homeschooling or in opposing it. One may take the *libertarian* view: the State has no right (or a very minimal right) to determine the conduct of its citizenry, and therefore parents or children desiring homeschooling should be allowed to practice that educational method if they so desire.

At the opposite end of the spectrum, there is the *statist* view: the State knows best and freedom of individual decision is allowable only where the State does not legislate. If, therefore, the State prohibits homeschooling, that is its right and the end of the matter.

Over against these two philosophies of individual-versus-State action, one encounters the approach of John Locke: there are "certain inalienable rights" possessed by individuals which neither the State, nor even the person herself, should be allowed to take away. Locke's viewpoint, based on historic Christian belief and biblical teaching concerning the creation of man in God's image, deeply influenced the American founding documents (especially the Declaration of Independence) and served as background for the modern human rights movement.[144]

If, however, the Lockeian position is seen as superior to the libertarian and the statist philosophies, the question immediately arises: *what is the specific content* of those rights deserving to be protected as inalienable? In

---

[143] *Ibid.* 2.

[144] Cf. John Warwick Montgomery, *Human Rights and Human Dignity*, 2d ed. (Calgary, Alberta: Canadian Institute for Law, Theology and Public Policy, 1995), *passim.*

terms of homeschooling, does the State's concern for the education of the citizenry constitute the right to prohibit homeschooling? Or does a parent's concern to ensure the best education for his offspring justify homeschooling as an inalienable right? And suppose the child wishes to be homeschooled: does the child have an absolute right to decide on the education she should have?

As for the State's right to educate, an important distinction needs to be made. One may well be able to argue that a properly educated populace is essential to a functioning State—particularly if one is thinking in terms of modern, representative democracies. But even if that right is conceded, it does not follow that the State has the right (a) to indoctrinate or (b) to determine and delimit the methods of educational instruction. As for indoctrination,

In matters of educational instruction the state must respect the philosophical and religious opinions of each person and this obligation applies equally in public and in private education. This requirement was included in the Protocol [No. 1 to the European Convention on Human Rights] as a result of clear evidence that during the Second World War totalitarian regimes had a powerful tendency to impose their ideological propaganda on the young, notably through cutting them off from the influence of their parents. Article 2 [of Protocol 1] therefore prohibits all forms of indoctrination of the young in the educational system and the parents themselves have the responsibility to see that this prohibition is carried out. It follows that the state's obligation to respect the philosophical and religious convictions of the parents prohibits all forms of indoctrination by the state.[145]

The Protocol referred to here reads as follows:

No person shall be denied the right to education. In the exercise of any functions which it assumes in relation to education and to teaching, the state shall respect the right of parents to ensure such education and teaching in conformity with their own religious and philosophical convictions.

It is worth pointing out that "indoctrination" need not (and in our modern, secular era, often is not) limited to sectarian religious ideas. Thus, were a state to impose "civil religion" (to employ sociologist Robert Bellah's expression) on its populace, this should be seen to run contrary to the European Convention—examples: teaching only an atheistic cosmology by re-

---

[145] Jean-Loup Charrier (ed.), *Code de la Convention Européenne des Droits de l'Homme* (Paris: Litec, 2005), 229 (our translation). Cited authority: *Graeme v. United Kingdom,* Application No. 13887/88 (5 February 1990, before the Commission), *DR* 64/158.

fusing to present intelligent design as a legitimate alternative; teaching only Darwinian evolutionary theory as if it were scientific fact and not subject to serious scientific criticism. A religion of secularism is as capable of indoctrination as traditional religious and denominational views—indeed, even more so today in our officially pluralist, but in fact very conformist times.

The Convention Protocol just quoted appears to defer to parental authority in the matter of education. Does this suggest that the parent has the inalienable right to determine the educational content and method for the instruction of her children? Surely not. Parents with anti-scientific convictions relating to the care of the body (e.g. Christian Scientists who oppose ordinary medical treatment, Jehovah's Witnesses who will not allow blood transfusion) are not able legally to keep their children from essential medical help. Likewise, the State has the right to establish minimal educational standards and to insist that all children conform to them. A parent who believes that his child will be hurt by mathematical instruction—or who wants him taught only the color blue—will not receive any support from the law.

And the child himself? Does the child, as subject of the educational process, have an inalienable right to determine the content and nature of that process? One might suppose so on the basis of a superficial application of the fundamental theme of the United Kingdom Children Act 1989 and the United Nations Declaration of the Rights of the Child—that "the best interests of the child" must be determinative. But those instruments clearly recognize that the child's wishes are not always equivalent to the child's best interests.[146] On the one hand, a child, owing to her immaturity, is not necessarily in a position to make reasonable or the best choices.[147]

Moreover, it is noteworthy that in the mature legal systems of today, adults, no less than children, are limited in their choice of conduct: they

---

[146] Cf. Andrew Bainham, *Children: The Modern Law,* 3d. rev. ed. (Bristol, England: Jordan Publishing/Family Law, 2005), especially 37 ff. and 70–72.

[147] A short but stimulating discussion of the philosophical issues pertaining to children's rights, including a treatment of "will theory" vs. MacCormick's sophisticated version of the "interest theory" of rights, may be found in Samuel Stoljar's *An Analysis of Rights* (London: Macmillan, 1984), 117–20. Stoljar suggests that the best justification of children's rights lies in "our human endeavour to replenish the human community." The inadequacy of this notion becomes immediately evident when we think of societies suffering from overpopulation or from inadequate natural resources: would we favor, for example, China's "one-child policy"—or a state's effort to control population by giving more rights to male children than to female children?

cannot do anything and everything they wish—even when the desired action would not harm others. Two examples are pertinent, one in the French, the other in the U.K. legal system. The "midget tossing" (*lancer de nains*) case in France involved a recreational pursuit in which dwarfs were competitively thrown into nets; the dwarfs were paid, were not injured, and wished to continue doing this. The highest French administrative court (*Conseil d'Etat*) ruled that the activity was an affront to the dignity of the human person and considered it irrelevant that the dwarfs did not themselves believe that their dignity was compromised.[148] The case was then taken to Strasbourg, but the Court declared it inadmissible, upholding the *Conseil d'Etat* judgment.[149] In the U.K., the famous "sado-masochist" case was decided along the same lines. The court ruled that sado-masochistic homosexual encounters occasioning actual bodily harm, even when consensual, were contrary to public morals and human values, and would not be permitted.[150] This case was also unsuccessfully brought to the European Court of Human Rights.[151]

Our conclusion at this point must be that neither the State, nor the parent, nor even the child has an unfettered right to determine educational content or method of instruction.

The European Court and Homeschooling

It is of more than passing interest that many of the articles of the European Convention are organized in two parts: Paragraph 1 sets forth the given right and Paragraph 2 allows limited qualification of that right by the State. Thus Article 9 (on religious freedom) states in Paragraph 1 that "everyone has the right to freedom of thought, conscience and religion"—and thus the right to worship, engage in public and private religious practices, and to change one's religion. This is followed by Paragraph 2 which indicates possible but limited exceptions: those "necessary in a democratic society in

---

[148] *Commune de Morsang-sur-Orge*, arrêt de 27 octobre 1995 (*Rec. Lebon*, p. 372). The case is particularly important because it established in French law that the dignity of the human person must be classed within the very concept of the *Ordre public*.

[149] *Wackenheim v. France*, Application No. 29961/96 (16 October 1996, before the Commission); the inadmissibility decision was unanimous.

[150] *R v. Brown* [1993] 2 All ER 75.

[151] *Laskey, Jaggard and Brown v.United Kingdom* [1997], Case No. 109/1995/615/703–705.

the interests of public safety, for the protection of public order, health or morals, or for the protection of the rights and freedoms of others."

The important point here is that *the right precedes the limitations*. In other words, the Court should on principle uphold the right *unless and until* it can be shown that a legitimate limitation exists to qualify that right. The limitations must never be allowed to swallow up the rights themselves.

There is no question that the Convention-guaranteed right of education is to be exercised by the State—in the sense that the State has the responsibility to establish minimal educational standards and to see that they are maintained. But does this mean that the State has the right to determine—and limit—the permissible *methods* by which such educational goals can be achieved? We argue that this is *not* the case.

The State has the right to insist on proper safety standards for travel. But who would argue that the State could therefore properly limit the means of transportation the public can use—monocycles, not bicycles; three-wheeled vehicles, not four-wheeled vehicles, etc.? The State can (and should) establish minimum standards for safe vehicles on the road, and owners should have to have their means of transport tested against those standards, but it is hardly appropriate for the State to tell the populace what kind of vehicle they can or cannot use.

In the case of homeschooling, the State has every right to insist that the child reach minimum educational levels through the schooling he or she receives. Thus, examinations or other objective evidences of intellectual attainment need to be required of all children at the appropriate educational levels. But the *means* by which the educational level is attained should not be a concern of the State. Where it is, the State clearly goes beyond its proper sphere and unnecessarily restricts the freedom of action of its citizenry.

In the *Family H. v. United Kingdom* case, Strasbourg significantly concluded:

> That to require the applicant parents to cooperate in the assessment of their children's educational standards by an education authority in order to ensure a certain level of literacy and numeracy, whilst, nevertheless, allowing them to educate their children at home, cannot be said to constitute a lack of respect for the applicant's rights under Article 2 of Protocol No. 1.[152]

---

[152] *Family H. v. United Kingdom,* Application No. 10233/83 (before the Commission), *D&R* 37 (1984), 106.

Comments a specialist: "It is interesting to note that the Commission does not attach so much weight to the form of the [primary] education, but rather to the responsibility of the State for its quality; a certain level of literacy and numeracy, leaving the rights of the parents unimpaired as much as possible."[153]

A state, however, may well claim (and, as we have seen in the *Konrad* matter, has claimed) that homeschooling is *socially* deleterious: that the homeschooled child is socially deprived. The State goes on to argue that the child needs to be integrated into a pluralistic society and its values. But as to alleged "social deprivation," the burden surely rests on the State to show that this is the case—a very difficult burden to discharge in light of the strong evidence of superior social skills on the part of homeschooled students in countries where homeschooling is permitted.

As for "the general interest of society to avoid the emergence of parallel societies based on separate philosophical convictions and the importance of integrating minorities into society" (to employ the language of the *Konrad* inadmissibility opinion), this surely smacks of political correctness—not education—and appears to fall squarely under the axe of indoctrination—which, as we have seen, is unqualifiedly condemned by Protocol 1, Article 2 of the European Convention. The function of an educational system is to bring the students to a proper level of knowledge, not to force them into a particular conception of society. To be sure, if homeschooling could be shown to contradict or denigrate the values of a democratic society, that would be sufficient reason to oppose it in that form, but, again, the burden of proof in demonstrating this should rest on the State, not on the student or his or her parents.

It is also worth emphasizing that "pluralism" must not deprive the citizens of the right to oppose viewpoints (even popular viewpoints) that are in fact false or evil. Cannibalism as a pluralistic option would not be a good idea, even on the ground of tolerance. Slavery was a contested idea before the American Civil War and, fortunately, the solution, as represented by the Emancipation Proclamation and amendments to the United States Constitution, was not to continue to tolerate both a slavery and an antislavery position on the question. A society must not become conformist to the point of not allowing homeschooling because the students are presented with values which may not jibe with what is regarded as officially *kosher*—so long as, one hastens to add, the students are confronted with the

---

[153]   P. van Dijk and G. J. H. van Hoof (eds.), *Theory and Practice of the European Convention on Human Rights,* 3rd ed. (The Hague, Netherlands: Kluwer Law International, 1998), 646.

variety of value systems characteristic of the modern world and are given the opportunity to make their own decisions as to the value system they prefer.

What we have here is not—though it may superficially appear to be such—an issue of "conflicting human rights norms": the State versus the individual.[154] There is nothing inherently in opposition between homeschooling and State interests—or between the rights of the child and the rights of the State. Potentially, if the State attempts to impose a "pluralistic" value system (whatever that means) on the family, or if the homeschooling is a covert attempt to undermine the society in which the child lives, there would indeed be an intolerable conflict. But there is no reason to suppose *a priori* that such conflicts exist, and if the State sticks to setting minimal educational standards—its proper function in this realm—and the homeschooling is educationally and socially responsible, there is no reason legally to refuse to allow it. And if the State believes that there is a problem, it is the State's burden to demonstrate it.

So, how should the European Court of Human Rights rule if and when a homeschooling case (uncontaminated by extrinsic considerations)[155] comes before it?

The starting point must surely be the Strasbourg Court's existing acquaintance with and commitment to the notion of a "law above the law," i.e., constitutional law and international law on a plane above ordinary legislation. The European Convention on Human Rights sets forth just such a higher law: a law taking precedence over ordinary, national legislation.

But the European Convention establishes only the right to education; it does not specify or limit the means to achieve it. What, then? Should the Strasbourg Court give untrammeled control to the State to limit educational methodology? Surely, not. The State has the responsibility to ensure that, however children are educated, they reach the proper level—and any schooling that does not attain that result must certainly be improved, or if that is not possible, abolished (for example, substandard public or private schools or incompetent homeschooling). But the burden rests on the State to show that there is the need to do this. Assuming *a priori* that a particular

---

[154] No mention of the homeschooling problem appears in Eva Brems (ed.), *Conflicts Between Fundamental Rights* (Antwerp, Belgium: Intersentia, 2008).

[155] Cases must not be taken to Strasbourg that muddy the issue of the legitimacy of home schooling *per se*. Thus it is a great error to go to Strasbourg with cases where homeschooling is intermixed with sincere but off-the-wall religious, ethical, and philosophical viewpoints; alleged procedural failings by local educational, social work, or police authorities; disciplinary, marital, and family problems; etc.

method of education is faulty is a meritless solution and flies in the face of democratic values.

Dr. Matthew Weait is undoubtedly correct when he writes:

> Contracting states [to the European Convention on Human Rights] are given a wide margin of appreciation to administer and finance their own systems of education. Successful challenges are likely to be scarce provided the system is both efficient *and sufficiently flexible to permit a reasonable measure of parental choice (through, for example, a diverse independent sector).*[156]

That is precisely the problem. When homeschooling is denied, the system may be said to lack the proper degree of flexibility; a reasonable measure of parental choice is denied; and a diverse independent educational sector ceases to have realistic meaning.

In spite of the great advances made by the European Court of Human Rights in bringing national law into conformity with first-generation human rights principles, there has been a pusillanimous tendency on the Court's part to defer to national legal systems where particularly controversial issues are at stake—for example, in the case of abortion, where the Court has left restrictions in place in conservative states but refused to mandate a right-to-life position in liberal countries.[157] Such an approach may be comprehensible on the ground that the Court needs to retain the confidence of the contracting states. However, the very idea of the Convention is to bring the laws of contracting states into line with fundamental human rights principles. Where the Convention is not explicit, the Court should never rule restrictively so as to reduce the scope of a general right. In the case of homeschooling, the Convention (as we have seen) sets forth the general principle that "the state shall respect the right of parents to ensure such education and teaching in conformity with their own religious and philosophical convictions." It must not, therefore, allow a contracting

---

[156] Matthew Weait, "Right to Education," *Human Rights Law and Practice,* ed. Lord Lester of Herne Hill and David Pannick, 2d ed. (London: LexisNexis UK, 2004), sec. 4.20, 471. Italics ours.

[157] "No consensus exists across Europe on the issue of abortion, and given the difficult moral and ethical issues involved, the Strasbourg organs have been understandably reluctant to pronounce substantively on whether the protection in art 2 [of the European Convention on Human Rights] for 'everyone' extends to the unborn child. In light of the differing national laws, a state will have a broad margin of appreciation with regard to the Convention on the issue of abortion" (Kay Taylor, "Right To Life," *ibid.,* sec. 4.2.17, 112).

state to eliminate a means of achieving this desired by parents—unless the state can show that the means in question is ineffective.

At the deepest level culturally, increasing secularism in modern society— particularly as manifested in Europe—poses special difficulties. The secular mindset can (as in the *Konrad* opinion) lead courts to an unconscious acceptance of politically correct notions of educational "integration."[158] Sadly, this also means that where constitutions and international human rights instruments are silent on an issue, the law will not appeal, as in the past, to the "higher law" as set out in the Holy Scriptures—the inalienable dignity of the human person, his family, and his personal decision-making, as John Locke derived these rights principally from biblical revelation—but will tend to defer to State power and bureaucracy, infused by prevailing pluralistic viewpoints. Where this occurs, the tragic result will be, not an increase in human rights protections but just the opposite. In that respect, the homeschooling issue may serve as a litmus test to discerning jurists.

---

[158] Michael Farris, chancellor of Patrick Henry College, has noted in a recent interview that a new wave of opposition to homeschooling seems to be on the horizon in the United States, based on the secular assumption that "Christian homeschooling parents are effectively transmitting values to their children that the elitists believe are dangerous to the well-being of both these very children and society as a whole." In this connection, Farris cites law professors from Northwestern University, George Washington University, and Emory University who have called for a ban on religious education in both private and homeschooling contexts (*Baptist Press*, 23 February 2011: http://www.bpnews.net [accessed 23 February 2011]). Also, in the United States—and in Europe as well—the refusal in many quarters to allow intelligent design to be offered as an alternative theory to Darwinian evolutionary models bespeaks of political correctness and ideological orthodoxy replacing educational openness and curricular flexibility (cf. *University of Montana Law Review*, April 2007).

APPENDIX

The Current Homeschool Situation in Sweden

by Michael P. Donnelly

Legal Yet Disfavored

This Appendix analyzes the situation for homeschooling families in Sweden and concludes with the stories of several who have left the country and some who have stayed to fight in court.

Before 2010, families who wished to homeschool in Sweden already faced a stringent set of regulations. Although the Swedish Education Act (1985:1100) of 1985 protected homeschooling as an alternative to compulsory school attendance, it required families to provide education that was equivalent to that taught in the public schools. In the 1990s, education was decentralized in Sweden, meaning that homeschooling families had to work with the 290 municipalities (kommun) now responsible for administering schools.[159]

The 1985 law allowed parents to fulfill the school obligation in ways other than public or private school. The law required permission to be given if the home education program was considered a fully satisfactory alternative to the education otherwise available to the child and if overseen by the authorities. In practice, families had to "apply" for permission, and local school authorities expected cooperation with whatever measures deemed necessary. By 2010, homeschooling in Sweden grew slowly. The number of homeschooling families remains estimated at about 100.

In 2004, a comprehensive review of the education law was initiated, and homeschooling was targeted for further restriction. Despite efforts to the contrary, a new education law was passed in 2010 with a significant and negative impact on home educating families. The new law permits homeschooling only under "exceptional circumstances" and also removes a key legal barrier to criminal prosecution of families who homeschool without permission.

---

[159] "Education in Sweden: A lesson for life," Sweden.se, http://www.sweden.se/eng/Home/Education/Basic-education/Facts/Education-in-Sweden/ (accessed October 24, 2011).

In advance of the law passing, local authorities anticipated the new regime in 2009 and began denying permission to a number of families in
various municipalities. These families took their cases to court, but were
almost universally denied permission to homeschool. In an interview during a nightly Swedish television segment, Swedish Minister for Education
Jan Björklund reflected the oppressive attitude of the Swedish government:

> [I]t is not voluntary to attend school in Sweden . . . Children have a right to
> attend school—yet there are a few parents, quite few, but they do exist, who
> think, 'This is wrong, this is something we are going to handle on our own.'
> I maintain that there is not a chance that parents could be able to teach [what
> is] taught in public school.[160]

Björklund further explained, "In junior high school, 16 different subjects
are taught. To educate a student at the junior high level requires many different teachers, who are experts in different subjects. In no way can a parent completely replace that education."[161] State Secretary to Björklund
Bertil Östberg also stated that homeschooling was a way to "circumvent"
the law in Sweden.[162]

The Swedish government described its motivation for the new language in
an explanatory introduction:

> Current school conventions make it clear that the education in school shall
> be comprehensive and objective, and thereby will be created so that all pu-
> pils can participate, no matter what religious or philosophical views the pupil
> or its legal guardian(s) may have. In accordance with this, it is the opinion of
> the Government that there is no need for a law to make homeschooling
> possible based on the religious or philosophical views of the family." [163]

---

[160] Video translation, HSLDA, http://www.hslda.org/hs/international/Sweden/201107
080.asp (accessed October 24, 2011). See also *Rapport* news segment that aired on
May 22, 2011, http://svt.se/.

[161] Ibid.

[162] "Hemundervisning ett sätt att kringgå reglerna," *Dagen*, August 19, 2010,
http://www.dagen.se/dagen/article.aspx?id=222274. See also "Östberg's comments moving Sweden down dangerous path," HSLDA, September 9, 2010,
http://www.hslda.org/hs/international/Sweden/201009090.asp (accessed October
24, 2011).

[163] Swedish Government Prop. 2009/10:165, 523. See also "How the Swedish Government voted against a human right," Rohus, http://rohus.nu/en/?English_informa
tion (accessed October 24, 2011).

In June 2009, the Ministry of Education and Research circulated the proposed law—entitled 'The New Education Act: for Knowledge, Choice and Security—to consultation bodies for comment.[164] The Ministry specifically asked Rohus, the Swedish Association for Home Education, for its comments; in response, the organization submitted a 228-page analysis of the law's effects on homeschooling, the family, and educational freedom. However, the Minister of Education repeatedly declined requests to meet with Rohus representatives to discuss their concerns. Rohus organized comprehensive efforts to stop the proposed law, including email campaigns and media coverage of homeschoolers via the newspapers and television. In the week leading up to the vote, the organization sent daily emails to all 349 Members of Parliament (MPs), each with a unique argument about the benefits of homeschooling.

In addition to pro-homeschool organizations, others in Sweden criticized the proposed law. The Swedish Supreme Court's advisory council reviewed the proposed law, as is standard practice, and declared the "exceptional circumstances" requirement for homeschooling "too vague."[165] Surrounded by controversy, the vote on the new education law was split from the beginning. MPs were required to vote on the law in totality and could not elect to vote against specific portions. As such, the Social Democrats, the Green Party, and the Leftist party that had originally proposed the dramatic changes for homeschoolers—when the overhaul of the law began in 2004—now opposed the law. MPs from these parties disliked changes such as increased control by the Minister of Education, the giving of performance grades at earlier ages, punishing bullies by simply moving them to another school, proposals to introduce more "school" and less play in daycare, and imposing more fines.[166] In the end, however, the sweeping education reform—all 1,500 pages—passed into law on June 22, 2010, an outcome guaranteed by the mandate of the government, the party line, and

---

[164] "The new Education Act—for knowledge, choice, and security," *Regeringskansliet*: Government Offices of Sweden, http://www.sweden.gov.se/sb/d/12996 (accessed October 24, 2011).

[165] Alex Newman, "Sweden Bans Home-schooling, Religious instruction," *New American*, June 28, 2010, http://www.thenewamerican.com/index.php/world-mainmenu-26/europe-mainmenu-35/3885-sweden-bans-home-schooling-religious-instruction (accessed October 24, 2011).

[166] "Swedes need help in final push to avoid extreme homeschool law," HSLDA, June 8, 2010, http://www.hslda.org/hs/international/Sweden/201006080.asp (accessed October 25, 2011).

bureaucratic procedures.[167] Only one MP from the ruling party voted against the proposed law. [168]

Although Swedish officials had many legitimate aims in reforming the country's decades-old education law, including the collection of various laws and regulations on education into one place and the creation of a more uniform structure, the overall effect of the new Education Act (2010:800) is to reduce both students' and parents' choice regarding education. Placing much more control in the hands of the government, the new law affects not only homeschoolers but all families in Sweden. The law now mandates a national curriculum and obliterates the notion of "independent" (or private) schools and school choice. With laws such as the Education Act increasingly encroaching upon individual freedom and responsibility, some have called Sweden a "reluctant democracy."[169]

Rohus President Jonas Himmelstrand expects the law to lead to civil disobedience or political exile on the part of homeschoolers. "The Swedish political authorities have deeply underestimated the convictions of Swedish homeschoolers," Himmelstrand said. "Most will not accept the new law."[170]

Sweden is a signatory to the United Nations Convention on the Rights of the Child. In correspondence with the Home School Legal Defense Association (HSLDA), the Swedish government stated that this convention is one of the reasons it has undertaken to regulate home education harshly. It appears that the Swedish government has interpreted its legal obligations under the treaty to include requiring that children go to a government school. The Convention does indeed state that children have a "right to an education," but it does not specify that education must be in a government school. In fact, by interpreting the word "education" in light of the principles of human rights as articulated in the United Nations Universal Declaration of Human Rights, this specification does not appear possible.

In a visit to Germany in 2006, a Special Rapporteur from the United Nations, Mr. Vernor Muñoz, wrote:

---

[167] "New education law makes homeschooling illegal," HSLDA, July 7, 2010, http://www.hslda.org/hs/international/Sweden/201007070.asp (accessed October 25, 2011).

[168] Ibid.

[169] "Sweden takes a hardening line," HSLDA, March 8, 2010, http://www.hslda.org/hs/international/Sweden/201003080.asp (accessed October 25, 2011).

[170] Newman, "Sweden Bans Home-schooling, Religious Instruction."

Education may not be reduced to mere school attendance and . . . educational processes should be strengthened to ensure that they always and primarily serve the best interests of the child. Distance learning methods and home schooling represent valid options which could be developed in certain circumstances, bearing in mind that parents have the right to choose the appropriate type of education for their children, as stipulated in article 13 of the International Covenant on Economic, Social and Cultural Rights. The promotion and development of a system of public, government-funded education should not entail the suppression of forms of education that do not require attendance at a school. In this context, the Special Rapporteur received complaints about threats to withdraw the parental rights of parents who chose home-schooling methods for their children.[171]

In the face of international human rights law and the statements of human rights investigators such as Mr. Muñoz regarding educational freedom, Sweden has taken a step away from human rights in the name of statist paternalism in education. The notion that government should determine what values are necessary for a democratic society and how they should be taught is totalitarian and should be rejected by a free, liberal democracy such as Sweden.

Documented Cases of Harsh Treatment of Homeschooling Families in Sweden

These families and cases are personally known to the author, who has provided the following case summaries.

Pettersson family (name changed to protect privacy)

After the local school headmaster denied the family permission to homeschool in late 2009, she threatened them with a social services investigation if the children did not immediately appear in school. The Petterssons waited for the school board to provide an explanation for the rejection of their application, but no explanation was supplied. Since the family had complied with existing Swedish law, they appealed the denial and accordingly declined to meet with school officials while the appeal was in process. Local school officials continued to doggedly pursue the family with numerous emails and letters. As of September 2010, the Pettersson's ap-

---

[171] Report of the Special Rapporteur on the right to education, Vernor Muñoz, UN General Assembly (A/HRC/4/29/Add.3), March 9, 2007.

peal was still unprocessed. After a year of their local school fighting them tooth and nail simply for choosing to teach their children at home, the family made the difficult decision to leave Sweden.[172]

Robbins family (name changed to protect privacy)

Despite the fact that the Robbins had successfully educated their son at home for the past six years, in autumn 2009 local authorities denied their application to homeschool. Authorities from the municipality demanded that their son begin to attend school immediately. In addition, the municipality fined each parent 10,000 Swedish kroner (approximately $1,500 in U.S. currency). When the family declined to pay or to send their son to the public school since the matter was in the hands of the court, officials sought a court order to force the family to render payment. In autumn 2010, officials also tried to deny due process to the family, arguing that since the municipality previously denied the family's right to homeschool, the family shouldn't get to argue their case in court again. The Robbins's case progressed through various levels of the Swedish court system as the family continued to appeal the decision. In January 2011, the family fled Sweden.[173]

Angerstig family

The Angerstig family currently homeschools their 13-year-old son, while their three other children attend local schools. Lisa Angerstig is an American who holds a master's degree in business and who is married to a Swede. In fall 2009, their municipality denied them permission to continue homeschooling. The Förvaltningsrätten, a lower administrative court, heard their case and agreed with the decision of the municipality. The verdict stated that their son had to go to school and that the parents would be fined as long as he stays home. Initial fines totaled around $1,400 USD. However, the family now receives fines for each day they homeschool, totaling over 80,000 Swedish kroner (about $12,500 USD). The family has appealed their case to a higher appeals court, the *Kammarrätten*, and has con-

---

[172] "Homeschoolers leave Sweden under pressure and protest," HSLDA, September 30, 2010, http://www.hslda.org/hs/international/Sweden/201009300.asp (accessed October 25, 2011).

[173] "Sweden denies due process to family, disregards legal system," HSLDA, October 25, 2010, http://www.hslda.org/hs/international/Sweden/201010250.asp (accessed October 25, 2011).

tinued to homeschool. This family has been featured in periodicals includ-ing *The Economist*, *Neo*, and other news publications.[174]

Himmelstrand family

The Himmelstrands had homeschooled their daughter, now 12 years old, for multiple years before the municipality denied them permission in 2008. Municipal officials still have not stated any obvious reason as to why their teaching is not adequate. The family currently faces fines approaching $40,000 USD. In the last three years, courts at multiple levels have either upheld the decision of the municipality or declined to hear the family's case. In a breakthrough in March 2011, the *Kammarrätten* appeals court agreed to take their case. Jonas Himmelstrand is the President of Rohus, the Swedish national homeschooling association, and travels internation-ally to speak about the ill effects of Sweden's family policies.[175]

Johansson family

The alarming case of Domenic Johansson offers a case study of the far-reaching effects of the new education law—both pre- and post-ratification. In the midst of the review of the education law in 2009, a seven-year old boy, Domenic Johansson, was forcibly removed from his parents, Christer and Annie, while the family was on board an airplane bound for Annie's homeland of India. Swedish police snatched Domenic without a warrant and placed him in state custody, but have not charged the Johanssons with a crime. Authorities have subsequently pointed to some minor dental prob-lems and a spotty vaccination history as justification for continuing to hold Dominic in state custody; this has persisted for more than two years. The Johansson family took the proper steps to inform their municipality of their intent to homeschool their son in preparation for their relocation. Munici-pal officials ignored normal procedure and did not meet with the family to assist them in pursuing home education; instead, the municipality fined

---

[174] "Homeschoolers vow to continue in face of new law," HSLDA, August 23, 2010, http://www.hslda.org/hs/international/Sweden/201008230.asp; "Continued battle for homeschooling," HSLDA, February 23, 2011, http://www.hslda.org/hs/internat ional/Sweden/201102231.asp (accessed October 25, 2011).

[175] "In breakthrough, Swedish appeals court to hear homeschooling case," HSLDA, March 25, 2011, http://www.hslda.org/hs/international/Sweden/201103250.asp (accessed October 25, 2011). See also "Hemundervisning på spel i rättsfall," *Världen idag*, March 17, 2010, http://www.varldenidag.se/nyhet/2010/03/17/Hem undervisning-pa-spel-i-rattsfall/ (accessed October 25, 2011).

them and referred the matter to the local court, with Swedish social services eventually authorizing what amounted to the kidnapping of Domenic.

Over the course of this tragic situation, the family has been denied due process and the right to choose an attorney of their choice, including two noted human rights attorneys.[176] As of October 2010, their case had been heard at the every level of the Swedish court system and the actions of social services upheld. With the assistance of HSLDA, the Alliance Defense Fund, and a Swedish human rights attorney, the family filed their application at the European Court of Human Rights (ECHR), their only remaining recourse. The ECHR finally assigned their application a case number in April 2011.[177]

Domenic is only allowed to visit with his parents once every five weeks, plus a supervised 15-minute telephone call once every two weeks. After tolerating this situation for nearly 18 months, Domenic's father took him home for a short but unapproved visit, and then spent two months in jail for his offense. In Christer Johansson's words: "The government has taken over my family, and now we are living in a nightmare."[178] Most recently, the social services authorities have filed for a termination of Annie and Christer's parental relationship to Domenic. This would permanently transfer parental custody to Domenic's current foster family.[179]

---

[176] "Sweden denies due process to family," HSLDA, June 14, 2010, http://www.hslda.org/hs/international/Sweden/201006140.asp; "Urgent action needed," HSLDA, December 13, 2010, http://www.hslda.org/hs/international/Sweden/201012130.asp (accessed October 25, 2011).

[177] "ECHR addresses Johansson case," HSLDA, April 2011, http://www.hslda.org/hs/international/Sweden/201104140.asp (accessed October 25, 2011).

[178] "Sweden—the next Germany for homeschoolers?" HSLDA, September 2009, http://www.hslda.org/hs/international/Sweden/200909160.asp (accessed October 25, 2011).

[179] "Officials seek to terminate Johansson parenthood," HSLDA, October 7, 2011, http://www.hslda.org/hs/international/Sweden/201110070.asp (accessed October 25, 2011).

About the Authors

This book contains papers presented by the authors at the XXV World Congress of Philosophy of Law and Social Philosophy 15–20 August, 2011, at Goethe University, Frankfurt am Main, Germany

Michael P. Donnelly, J.D., is a staff attorney and the Director for International Relations at the Home School Legal Defense Association and Adjunct Professor of Government at Patrick Henry College in Virginia, U.S.A. He serves thousands of families in 8 states and 200 countries, helping them to resolve disputes with authorities related to home education. Donnelly and his wife are homeschooling parents of seven. Donnelly is a member of the Massachusetts, New Hampshire, District of Columbia, and West Virginia state bars, as well as the U.S Supreme Court bar. Websites: www.hslda.org and www.phc.edu

Thomas Schirrmacher, Dr. phil, Dr. theol., Ph.D., is Professor of the Sociology of Religion at State University of the West, Timisoara, Romania; Director of the World Evangelical Alliance's International Institute for Religious Freedom (Bonn, Cape Town, and Colombo); and author of more than 80 books translated into 17 languages, among them "Human Rights", "Human Traffoickung", "Racism", "Fundamentalism" and a research paper on homescholling written for the educational department of the State University of Bonn. His article in this book was translated from German by Dr. Richard McClary.

John Warwick Montgomery, Ph.D., D. Théol., LL.D., is Distinguished Research Professor of Philosophy and Christian Thought at Patrick Henry College and Professor Emeritus at the University of Bedfordshire, England. His degrees include a Ph.D. (Chicago), D.Théol. (Strasbourg, France), and LL.D. (Cardiff, Wales, U.K.). He is a member of the California, District of Columbia, Virginia, and Washington state bars, as well as the U.S. Supreme Court bar. In addition, he is a Barrister-at-Law in England and Wales and an Avocat à la Cour in Paris. Websites: www.jwm.christendom. co.uk, www.apologeticsacademy.eu, and www.ciltpp.com

www.ingramcontent.com/pod-product-compliance
Lightning Source LLC
Chambersburg PA
CBHW071333210526
45161CB00006B/34